THE BEST OF

CHEF

AT

HOME

whitecap

THE BEST OF
CHEF
AT
HOME

ESSENTIAL RECIPES FOR TODAY'S KITCHEN

CHEF MICHAEL SMITH

PHOTOGRAPHY BY JAMES INGRAM

Whitecap Books is known for its expertise in the cookbook market, and has produced some of the
most innovative and familiar titles found in kitchens across North America. Visit our website at
www.whitecap.ca.

Food photography: James Ingram, Jive Photographic
Author photograph on page ix: James Ingram
Additional photography: Loretta Campbell, Eastern Eyes Photography
Food styling and props: Patti Hetherington
Food production: Justin Ford and Gregory Campbell
Food photographer's assistants: Beth Dunham and Alison Beckett
Recipe testing: Maureen Campbell
Editor: Melva McLean
Proofreader: Ann-Marie Metten
Cover design: Mauve Pagé and Michelle Mayne
Cover photography: Tracey Kusiewicz
Photographs on the refrigerator and on the front and back flaps: James Ingram
Interior design: Mauve Pagé
Illustrations: Chef Michael Smith

Printed in China

Library and Archives Canada Cataloguing in Publication

Smith, Michael, 1966-
    The best of Chef at home / Michael Smith.

ISBN 978-1-55285-984-1
    1. Cookery. I. Title.

TX714.S594 2009   641.5   C2009-902673-2

The publisher acknowledges the financial support of the Canada Council for the Arts, the British
Columbia Arts Council and the Government of Canada through the Book Publishing Industry
Development Program (BPIDP). Whitecap Books also acknowledges the financial support of the
Province of British Columbia through the Book Publishing Tax Credit.

10 11 12 13 5

This book is inspired by Rachel and Gabe, and by anyone who's ever eaten at our table. It reflects our family's ongoing food journey and the spirit of our home kitchen. It's for any cook who enjoys sharing healthy, spontaneous flavours with their family and friends.

CONTENTS

INTRODUCTION

The Best of Chef at Home is more than just a cookbook; it's a guidebook to help you freestyle as you cook. Included are all the essential recipes you'll need to impress yourself in your own kitchen. While the gold standard recipes will be useful every day of the week, each is just a starting point. The secret to successful freestyle cooking is to combine your own creativity with the basic idea and instinctive insight within each recipe.

A table full of local flavour and creative energy is one of life's great miracles. There are few things as powerful and rewarding as cooking a simple meal and then sharing it with your family and friends, especially when you enjoy the act of creation. That satisfaction is what makes freestyle cooking so much fun!

Freestyling means that cooking can be whatever you want it to be. Life swirls by, challenges pile up and cooking becomes a chore, a stressful necessity. Or life slows down and cooking becomes a pleasant interlude, a hobby or even a passion. In your kitchen, the choice is yours.

You don't have to be a scientist, nutritionist or chef to be a great cook. Your food doesn't have to be picture perfect, enticingly exotic or new and exciting. Great cooking is simply about relaxing in the kitchen, enjoying the process and losing yourself in the moment. If the cook is having a great time, then so is everyone else. And the best way to have fun while you're cooking is to freestyle your way to flavour!

FREESTYLE COOKING

There are as many ways to cook as there are cooks. Some of us embark on endless searches for the perfect recipe and then scrutinize it with a microscope, obsess over the difference between sweet potatoes and yams, and finely chopped versus minced, while laser levelling our cupfuls. Some glance at the picture, slam the book shut, throw caution to the wind and with the ingredients produce seemingly effortless masterpieces that barely resemble the original recipe. It's a lot more fun to let loose and freestyle your way to flavour. The key is how we use recipes.

Written recipes are useful cooking tools. They give us confidence in the kitchen. They help us write shopping lists and serve as a reference, reminding us of amounts and procedures. Their artful pictures inspire us to cook and

give us a sense of what we're striving for. Sometimes they even tell a story and give us historical information. But even the very best recipe is just words on paper until it comes alive in the hands of a cook.

When you freestyle with a recipe, you make it your own. You personalize it. You stir in your own ideas and flavours. When you freestyle, you use a recipe as a launching point without feeling constrained by its

limitations. Recipes become constraining when we allow them to define the success of our cooking. Their precise ingredient lists and exacting measures seem to suggest that any deviation will result in clouds of smoke and ruinous take-out bills. The secret is to think of each recipe as a road map and not a chauffeur. The journey is a lot more fun when you're in the driver's seat, and the destination will be tastier when you arrive.

To inspire your creativity, the recipes in this book include two different types of information: the basic ingredients and steps you need to get started and lots of empowering insight—the why behind the how. The recipes also include suggestions on how you can modify, change, evolve, alter, adjust and transform your way to successful freestyling!

HOW TO BE A CHEF AT HOME

Your kitchen is your artist's studio
Cooking is as much an art form as you choose to make it so immersing yourself in an inspiring artistic space can really add to the enjoyment. Take the time to straighten up, get rid of last night's dishes, pour a glass of your favourite wine, crank the tunes and enjoy the moment.

Cook with insight
Think about the steps ahead. Read the recipe and absorb the hints on why a particular method or technique works best for the ingredients. Understand that every ingredient is full of flavours waiting to be coaxed forward by great cooking. It'll help you understand why one ingredient goes with another, when something's done cooking or why a certain ingredient is always handled the same way.

Measure loosely
With the exception of baking, most recipes don't rely on rigid precision to be successful. When measurements aren't flexible, recipes are too uptight. If they're too specific, they seem to suggest that there's only one way to cook—the writer's way. Not true! Your idea of a spoonful or a dash may be different from mine but that's the point. Any two cooks will get different results from the same recipe but yours will be personalized with your own kitchen spirit.

Be bold
Most seasoning mistakes are made by adding too little of a particular flavour instead of too much. It's human nature to take baby steps into the unknown. I understand. But don't be tentative. Cooking is a lot more fun—and flavourful—when you throw caution to the wind.

Experiment
Every recipe in this book is ripe for experimentation. There may be a few steps that need to be done a specific way, but you'll also find many steps that can be modified as you please. Play with your ingredients—substitute one for another—and you'll find all kinds of fun variations that'll belong to you. You'll realize that words on paper are no substitute for flavours on the plate.

Don't cook a dish the same way twice

Who says a great dish has to taste the same way every time you make it? Not me! That's boring. You can certainly repeat a flavour combination you enjoy, but a recipe doesn't need to be rigid to be perfect. I constantly tinker with amounts and look for ways to vary a dish I've gotten comfortable with.

Cook like a chef

You don't have to be a pro to be inspired by a chef, but using the right tools does help. For example, using a microplane grater to create frozen ginger powder, freshly grated nutmeg or a fragrant pile of lemon zest is a flavour revelation. An immersion blender is fast and efficient and easy to clean too. Freestyling your way to the table—trying new ingredients and techniques— is much more fun and entertaining than blindly following a recipe.

Focus on flavour

Every moment, every nuance and every decision you make in the kitchen affects flavour. The methods and techniques of cooking are not arbitrary; they've evolved from every cook's instinctive desire to create healthy, fla-vourful food. You can develop your own freestyling approach by looking for the insight beyond the idea and adding flavour at every turn.

You can taste patience

Cooking is at its best when it unfolds at its own pace. Life has its own time-line but it doesn't always have to overshadow the process in your kitchen. You can take your time, relax, be in the moment and watch as time fades away and things happen as they need to. You don't have to rush to cook quickly.

Share your best with family and friends

Your food is best when it's shared. When this spirit permeates the creative process, it adds flavour and colour. You may be in the kitchen simply because someone has to cook, but you can still choose to infuse your food with your spirit by sharing your best.

Dishwashing is the ultimate adventure

In my house we have a great deal. When Rachel cooks, I clean up. When I cook, I clean up. Let's just say I know a thing or two about washing dishes. Sure, you can enlist a supporter or two and outsource the inevitable scullery shift, but there's honour and integrity to be found when you do it yourself. Few things in life are as gratifying as facing down a pile of dirty dishes, diving in and prevailing against all odds.

THE SUSTAINABLE KITCHEN

All of us share an instinctive concern for the health of our collective environment. Every day one of the best places in your world to make enlightened, sustainable choices is your kitchen. Your food choices matter!

Create a healthy food lifestyle

The whole point of cooking is to create healthy food to sustain your family and friends. An energetic devotion to their physical and spiritual wellness is a fundamental part of all great cooking because nutrition, simplicity and flavour are closely linked. Just taking the time to cook for yourself—rather than consuming spirit-draining factory food—is a powerful and positive decision. Colourful variety, balanced choices and realistic habits are all part of a healthy food lifestyle.

Be a good neighbour: support your local farmers and food artisans

Locally sourcing as many of your ingredients as possible helps connect you to time and place. First, local ingredients taste better. That's being good to you! Second, a strong local food connection allows you to share your hard-earned money directly with farmers. That's just being good to your neighbours. And transporting local ingredients from the farmer's fields to your table takes less time and less fuel. That's just being good to your Earth!

Choose your ingredients responsibly

It's not always possible to choose local ingredients but it's always possible to choose them responsibly. Avoid processed food; ounce for ounce, it uses dramatically more energy than simply cooking for yourself. Limit the amount of meat you consume—it's better for you and the environment. Choose seafood from sustainable fisheries. Organic ingredients are always better for the environment but also for your family and the families that helped produce them. The most important thing you can do is get engaged. Don't take your food for granted. How you eat and what you eat can profoundly affect your personal environmental legacy.

This book contains all the basic recipes any cook needs up his or her sleeve. Each recipe is presented in a way that gives you the basic information you need to get cooking, as well as the insight that makes the journey easier and the destination tastier, so as you cook, you can feel free to play. Here are a few things to keep in mind as you do.

Know your ingredients

If a recipe is not specific about what type of ingredient to use, feel free to use any kind. An onion is an onion no matter what colour or size it is. Whatever you happen to have on hand will taste great. In general, I prefer the bright flavours of fresh herbs to the often-dull flavours of dried ones. I use corn or canola oil for all-purpose cooking unless I specify flavourful olive oil. I tend to use organic products whenever possible; they might cost a bit more, but their tasty goodness is worth it. If I ask you to use your favourite ingredient, pick the tastiest one you can find. If the instructions seem flexible, you can trust that whatever you choose will work just fine and taste even better.

Spoonfuls

Most of the recipes in this book ask you to use precise teaspoon and tablespoon measurements, but please don't think that rigid measuring is the only way to precise flavour. It's not! Instead, feel free to use your own judgment. Use a small spoon for less flavour or a big heaping one if you like. This is especially true with aromatic ingredients like spices and herbs.

Feel the temperature

You'll notice that I suggest a medium-high heat in many of the recipes. I usually don't cook with the highest heat setting on my stove because it burns things. High heat is really only good for boiling water. There's a magical sweet spot on every dial that's perfect for caramelizing and browning the simple sugars in almost all of the food you cook. Find it, and you'll never burn a chicken breast or a pancake again.

Season like a pro

Salt and pepper are your best friends in the kitchen. They make the ordinary extraordinary. I don't like the chemical flavours of iodized table salt so I use crisp, clean sea salt or coarse Kosher salt. Use a pepper grinder to add the spicy heat, and often overlooked aromatic flavour, of freshly ground pepper. Lightly season ingredients as they cook, then taste them when they're done and season again before serving.

Taste

The best lesson I can pass on to you from all my years of cooking is to taste food as you cook it, not just when it's done. At first, you'll take note of general flavours, but with practice, you'll gain important insight into what happens to ingredients as you cook them. Taste everything!

STARTERS & SNACKS

WHOLE GRAIN PANCAKES — 3

CHEDDAR CHEESE OMELETTE — 4

COUNTRY INN GRANOLA — 7

CHUNKY MONKEY — 9

GRILLED CHEESE SANDWICH — 10

TUNA FISH SANDWICH — 13

SMOKED SALMON HORS D'OEUVRES — 14

TOMATO BASIL BRUSCHETTA — 16

HUMMUS & PITA CHIPS — 19

OLIVE OIL POPCORN — 20

WHOLE GRAIN PANCAKES

This favourite flavour is first in many ways, for this chapter, for this book and often for our first heat, the first cooking of the day for my family. A batch of these pancakes is a great way to spin a strong dose of whole grains into a get-out-of-bed treat and to kick-start a nutritious day. SERVES 4

1 cup (250 mL) of unbleached
   all-purpose flour
1 cup (250 mL) of whole wheat,
   grain or almond flour
1 cup (250 mL) of oatmeal flakes
2 tablespoons (30 mL) of baking
   powder
1 teaspoon (5 mL) of ground
   cinnamon or nutmeg

½ teaspoon (2 mL) of salt
2 cups (500 mL) of any milk or water
¼ cup (60 mL) of vegetable oil
   or melted butter
2 tablespoons (30 mL) of honey
2 eggs, 4 for added richness
1 teaspoon (5 mL) or more of pure
   vanilla extract

A preheated pan is the first secret to pancake perfection. While you mix the batter, preheat your largest, heaviest skillet over your sweet spot, the medium to medium-high heat that gives the batter time to cook through while the surface browns. Your preheated skillet is at the perfect temperature when a few scattered water drops dance on it (just right) without evaporating (too hot) or just pooling still and simmering (too cool).

Whisk together the flours, oatmeal flakes, baking powder, cinnamon, salt and brown sugar, if using (see Variation), to distribute the fine powders evenly among the coarser ones.

Whisk together the milk or water, oil or butter, honey, eggs and vanilla and then pour them into the bowl of dry ingredients. Lose the whisk and grab a wooden spoon that won't clog in the batter. Stir the batter until it is smooth, but don't overmix.

Spoon the batter into the preheated pan, evenly filling it with a lot of little pancakes or a few large ones. Smaller ones are easier to flip and are easy to pass out to a hungry crowd.

Watch for bubbles. As the batter heats through, the baking powder will activate and release leavening bubbles that rise to the surface. Keep an eye on them. At first, they'll burst and disappear, but as the batter cooks through they'll leave behind a telltale hole.

When the pancakes are evenly covered here and there with holes, it's time to flip. Because the batter is heated through, and the first side is already browned, the second side cooks faster.

You can get ahead of a crowd by stashing a plate full of pancakes in a warm oven. Cover the plate with a bowl, and they'll stay fresh and warm while you cook more.

> Because the batter has very little refined white flour in it, it can take lots of stirring without "toughening." White flours are high in gluten, which gives bread dough strength, but toughens muffins, cakes and pancakes. Oatmeal, almond and other grain flours don't contain gluten and are ground fine enough to support the batter. They're also great for adding extra flavour, richness and nutrition.

Freestyle VARIATION

The first 3 cups (750 mL) of flours and grains can easily be custom blended. Use any mixture you like as long as it measures 3 cups (750 mL) in total. You may also use any milk, like cow, soy, rice or a blend. Honey adds lots of complex aromatic flavour but you can also add ½ cup (125 mL) brown or white sugar to the dry ingredients. If you like experimenting with spices, you can brand every batch with a new name and a new spice flavour. Simply varying your choice of spice completely changes the flavour of the pancakes. Just for aromatic kicks!

CHEDDAR CHEESE OMELETTE

An omelette is a great way to start your day, but it's also right at home on the dinner table. Farm-fresh eggs, cheddar cheese and aromatic herbs are all you need to create an elegant, simple meal. Some purists insist that the perfect omelette must never colour, but I prefer the flavour that a touch of browning adds. SERVES 1

3 eggs
½ cup (125 mL) of shredded aged
   cheddar cheese
1 teaspoon (5 mL) of freshly
   minced thyme

1 green onion (green top and white
   bottom), thinly sliced
a sprinkle or two of sea salt and
   freshly ground pepper
vegetable oil
1 teaspoon (5 mL) of butter

You may use any of your favourite cheeses in this omelette. Tarragon, basil, oregano and simple parsley all taste great too. Instead of your favourite herb try a spoonful of pesto. (See page 246 for a recipe for Basil Pesto.)

Preheat a heavy sauté pan over medium-high heat.

Vigorously whisk the eggs together until they're very well combined. Whisk in the cheese, thyme, green onion and salt and pepper.

Add a splash of oil to the pan, enough to cover the bottom with a light film. Drop the butter into the centre of the oil. It will begin to melt and sputter but won't immediately burn. The oil protects it from the direct heat of the pan so you'll get brown butter flavour but not blackened butter.

Pour the eggs into the centre of the pan. Let them sear, sizzle and brown for a moment or two. Browning it now is your best chance to add some caramelized flavour to your omelette. Gently stir the eggs for a few moments until they seem almost fully cooked. Form into an even round omelette shape and let it continue to cook for a few moments, lightly browning the bottom.

Lift the pan, allowing the far edge to droop a bit. In one continuous motion, deftly flip the omelette over. If you're still mastering your flip you may also use a spatula.

Continue heating for a few more moments until the omelette is cooked through. Slide it out of the pan onto your plate, folding it into a half-moon shape as you do. With a hot pan it will take about 2 minutes in total to cook the omelette.

COUNTRY INN GRANOLA

When I was a country inn chef, my guests loved starting their day with a bowl of this great-tasting homemade granola. It was one of my most popular recipes. Packed full of nuts, seeds, fruit and whole-grain goodness, it's hospitable and healthy. Your own homemade breakfast cereal beats the camouflaged candy at your supermarket any day of the week. MAKES 4 LB (1.8 KG) OR 16 SERVINGS

1 cup (250 mL) of honey
1 cup (250 mL) of vegetable oil
1 tablespoon (15 mL) of ground cinnamon
1 teaspoon (5 mL) of ground nutmeg
1 teaspoon (5 mL) of pure vanilla extract
8 cups (2 L) of rolled oats
1 cup (250 mL) of wheat germ

1 cup (250 mL) of wheat bran
1 cup (250 mL) of flax meal
1 cup (250 mL) of unsalted sunflower seeds
1 cup (250 mL) of almond slivers
1 cup (250 mL) of chopped walnuts
1 teaspoon (5 mL) of salt
2 cups (500 mL) of raisins or sweetened dried cranberries

Preheat your oven to a gentle browning temperature—325°F (160°C)—hot enough to toast the granola but not hot enough to burn it.

Pour the honey, oil, cinnamon, nutmeg and vanilla into a saucepan and bring them to a simmer over medium heat. Gentle heating brightens the flavours of the spices and melts the normally thick honey, so it combines evenly with the dry ingredients.

Toss together the oats, wheat germ, wheat bran, flax meal, sunflower seeds, almonds, walnuts and salt until they're evenly combined. When the oil mixture is hot, pour it over the dry ingredient mixture. Stir well until everything is evenly coated.

Spread the raw granola into a single even layer on a rimmed baking sheet or two. Bake for 40 minutes or so, until the oats are evenly toasted. Every 10 minutes or so, stir the works to help it cook evenly. Continue baking and stirring until the granola is baked golden brown.

Rest at room temperature until completely cool, then stir in the raisins (or cranberries).

Granola can be stored in an airtight container for up to a week.

freestyle VARIATION

Other than the basic oats, if you're missing a dry ingredient or two, you can still carry on. Feel free to add any combination of your favourite nuts, seeds or dried fruits. There are many to choose from. Try varying the spice blend too: cardamom and ginger work well. You may substitute maple syrup for the honey.

CHUNKY MONKEY

This fun snack is a tasty way to add some healthy flavour to a lunchbox or your table. It's one of our family favourites partly because it's so easy to make. SERVES 1 OR 2

2 tablespoons (30 mL) of chunky
   peanut butter

1 whole wheat tortilla
1 ripe banana

Spread an even layer of peanut butter on the tortilla. Lay the banana towards the bottom, straightening it slightly to remove its curve. Tightly roll the tortilla around the banana.

   Slice into rounds and serve.

You may use any peanut butter you like. Nut butters like cashew and almond also work very well. For a classic flavour treat, add a thin layer of your favourite jelly.

GRILLED CHEESE SANDWICH

You don't really need a recipe to make a great grilled cheese sandwich. Some great cheese, hearty bread and a bit of butter will do just fine. You can also easily finesse this humble snack into a classic treat by adding some of your favourite personalized flavours. MAKES 2 SANDWICHES

4 slices of your favourite
    sandwich bread
4 slices of aged cheddar cheese

1 tablespoon (15 mL) or so of
    butter, softened

Aged cheddar cheese is the gold standard for a great grilled cheese sandwich, but you can use any good melting cheese. Try experimenting until you find a favourite—Swiss, Gouda and havarti are all very good. Try including a few slices of crisp bacon, sliced ham or ripe tomato. You can even make a pizza sandwich with mozzarella and a spoonful of tomato sauce. For an extra special treat, try Cambozola cheese with freshly cracked black pepper and orange marmalade.

Preheat a heavy sauté pan over medium heat—not too hot or the bread will burn before the cheese has a chance to melt.

Sandwich the bread and cheese together. Lightly butter both sides of the sandwich and position in the warm pan.

Slowly and patiently brown the sandwich on 1 side until golden brown and beautiful. Flip. Brown the second side and then serve immediately. A grilled cheese sandwich is at its best while the cheese is still hot and oozing!

TUNA FISH SANDWICH

When I was a little boy a tuna sandwich was the very first thing I was allowed to make all by myself in the kitchen. I was very proud that I didn't need a helping hand—or a recipe! I know that you don't either, so think of this as a guided tour to jazzing up this kitchen classic with a few new flavours.

MAKES 2 SANDWICHES

one 6 oz (170 g) can of water-
   packed tuna
a squeeze or two of lemon juice
a generous splash of your best olive oil
1 tablespoon (15 mL) of Dijon mustard
1 tablespoon (15 mL) of minced red
   or green onion
1 tablespoon (15 mL) of minced celery

1 tablespoon (15 mL) of chopped
   parsley
a sprinkle or two of sea salt
   and freshly ground pepper
4 slices of whole wheat bread
a few lettuce leaves
a handful of potato chips

Flake the tuna with a fork and then mix it with the lemon juice, olive oil, mustard, onion, celery and parsley. Unlike bland mayonnaise, olive oil will add lots of rich peppery flavour. Have a taste and then season to your liking with salt and pepper.

Spread a thick layer of the tuna salad on 2 slices of bread. Top with a layer of lettuce and crisp potato chips. Slap on the remaining bread. Press down a bit to even out the chips, then have a huge bite. Remember to share the other one!

All canned tuna fish is good for you, but I prefer water-packed to oil-packed, and skipjack or "light" because it has less mercury than albacore or "white" tuna. Either chunky or solid tuna are fine because you'll be flaking it anyway.

A great sandwich can be quickly and easily made with whatever's in your kitchen. If you don't have lemon, a splash of any vinegar will add a bit of sharp flavour contrast. Any type of mustard or onion works well too. I like to try fresh herbs other than parsley; tarragon and dill are two of my favourites. I sometimes add cucumber or even vegetable sprouts. Of course, any bread will work too; try toasting it for a bit more crunch. Whatever you do though, make sure you try the chips!

SMOKED SALMON HORS D'OEUVRES

Smoked salmon is the ultimate party guest. It's versatile, gets along with lots of other ingredients and always adds a luxurious twist to the proceedings. It's also easy to work with because you're limited only by your imagination.

MAKES 20 PIECES

12 to 16 slices of smoked salmon	1 tablespoon (15 mL) of mustard
½ cup (125 mL) of softened cream cheese	2 green onions, thinly sliced
	20 whole grain crackers

You may try seasoning or garnishing the smoked salmon purée with any one of your favourite fresh herbs. Dill, basil, parsley and even cilantro all work well. A spoonful of pesto is very flavourful too. If you have any of the filling left over, it can easily be served as a tasty dip.

On your work surface, lay out an 18- × 12-inch (45 × 30 cm) piece of plastic wrap. In the centre of the plastic, overlap 8 pieces or so of smoked salmon to form a rectangle about 12 × 8 inches (30 × 20 cm).

Toss the remaining smoked salmon, cream cheese, mustard and green onions into your food processor. Purée until smooth enough to spread an even layer of the mixture on the smoked salmon slices, leaving about 1 inch (2.5 cm) of 1 long edge uncovered.

Starting at the long edge that's covered with the cream cheese mixture, roll the smoked salmon into a tight log. Pick up the plastic wrap and use it to encourage the salmon to roll tightly. The uncovered edge at the top will help form a tight seal. Pinch the plastic wrap on both ends and then roll the log until it tightens and forms a cylinder.

Refrigerate or freeze for several hours to help it firm. When the roll is firm enough to cut, slice it into even rounds. Place each round on a cracker, sprinkle your favourite garnish on top (see Variation) and serve.

TOMATO BASIL BRUSCHETTA

There are as many ways to pile flavour on a slice of crisp bread as there are cooks. Here are some ideas to help you find your favourite! MAKES 16 PIECES

4 thick slices of rustic bread
a splash or two of your best olive oil
2 large cloves of garlic, each cut in half
1 cup (250 mL) or so of shredded
    mozzarella cheese
2 or 3 ripe local tomatoes

a handful of fresh basil leaves,
    finely sliced or chopped
2 or 3 green onions, finely sliced
a sprinkle or two of sea salt
    and freshly ground pepper

Freestyle VARIATION

You can add any flavour you like to the tomato mixture. Try looking to the Mediterranean for inspiration. Olives, capers, artichokes and sun-dried tomatoes are all great ideas. Besides basil, any fresh herb or pesto works well. For an interesting and tasty twist, try using ripe, local strawberries instead of tomatoes.

Preheat your barbecue or broiler.

Generously brush each slice of bread with olive oil, and grill or toast it until golden brown on both sides.

Vigorously rub both sides of the toasted bread with the garlic, dramatically scenting each slice. Sprinkle some of the mozzarella cheese on each slice of bread and return it to the grill or broiler for a few moments, just long enough to melt the cheese a bit.

Cut each slice into quarters.

Chop the tomatoes and toss them with the basil leaves and green onions. Season the mixture with salt and pepper. Place a spoonful on top of each bread slice.

HUMMUS & PITA CHIPS

In Arabic, the word "hummus" means chickpeas. In the world of food, hummus is a dip or spread made from a purée of chickpeas, tahini, lemon, olive oil and garlic. It's very easy to make, very tasty and very healthy. It's a convenient snack—especially with crisp pita chips—and a frequent guest at our table.

MAKES ABOUT 2 CUPS (500 ML)

4 pitas
1 tablespoon (15 mL) or so of your
    best olive oil
a sprinkle or two of sea salt and freshly
    ground pepper
one 19 oz (540 mL) can of chickpeas,
    drained and rinsed
¼ cup (60 mL) of tahini (sesame
    paste)

zest and juice of 1 lemon
2 cloves of garlic, finely minced
2 more tablespoons (30 mL)
    of olive oil
another sprinkle or two of sea salt and
    freshly ground pepper
a splash of olive oil
a sprinkle of paprika
a sprinkle of chopped parsley

Preheat your oven to 350°F (180°C).

Brush each pita with olive oil and then sprinkle with salt and pepper. Cut into 6 or 8 pie-shaped wedges. Arrange the pieces on a baking tray and bake until toasted and crisp, about 15 minutes or so.

Toss the drained chickpeas into your food processor or blender. Add the tahini, lemon zest and juice, garlic and the last 2 tablespoons (30 mL) of olive oil. Purée until smooth, adding a splash or two of water, or more olive oil, to reach a soft creamy texture. Taste and season with salt and pepper as you like.

{ Draining and rinsing the chickpeas really well will not remove any nutrients, but it will remove any lingering processed taste.

To serve hummus, splash it with some olive oil, and sprinkle paprika and/ or chopped parsley on top.

Hummus is one of the most common foods in the Middle East, and every cook has his or her own version. To create yours, try adding more or less of the tahini, lemon zest and juice, garlic or olive oil. You may also add other ingredients like olives, capers, sun-dried tomatoes, pesto, parsley, chives, green onions or the traditional ground cumin. The pita chips may also be dusted with any herb or spice before baking.

OLIVE OIL POPCORN

Popcorn is the perfect snack. It's whole-grain healthy, addictively tasty and easy to experiment with. It's traditional to toss it with lots of melted butter, but you'll find that olive oil works just as well—and it's a lot better for you.

MAKES 4 TO 5 CUPS (1 TO 1.25 L)

2 tablespoons (30 mL) of your
   best olive oil
½ cup (125 mL) of popcorn kernels

a sprinkle or two of sea salt
   and freshly ground pepper
2 more tablespoons (30 mL)
   of olive oil

Pour the first 2 tablespoons (30 mL) of olive oil into a 3- or 4-quart (3 or 4 L) pot set over high heat. Add the popcorn and shake the pan to evenly distribute it into 1 thin layer.

Continue heating until the first kernel or two pops. Cover the pot with a lid or sauté pan, leaving a gap for the steam to escape so the popcorn doesn't get soggy.

Listen to the popcorn. It will gradually increase in cadence until it's popping continuously. Eventually it will start to slow down. When it does, turn the heat down to low, and after a minute or two it will stop popping. Turn off the heat and generously season the popcorn with salt and pepper. Splash in the second 2 tablespoons (30 mL) of olive oil. Toss everything together until combined well. The olive oil will help the seasoning adhere.

freestyle VARIATION

For a "grown up" version, toss popcorn with ½ teaspoon (2 mL) or so of any aromatic herb or spice you care to try. Ground cumin, cinnamon, thyme, rosemary and paprika are all excellent choices. For a savoury twist, try grated Parmesan cheese or garlic powder. For a sweet treat, try adding ½ teaspoon (2 mL) each of sugar and cocoa powder.

SOUPS

HOMEMADE CHICKEN BROTH — 24
CHICKEN NOODLE SOUP — 27
CREAM OF MUSHROOM SOUP — 28
FRENCH ONION SOUP — 31
LOUISIANA SHRIMP GUMBO — 32
MARITIME CLAM CHOWDER — 34
MUSHROOM MISO BROTH WITH BUCKWHEAT NOODLES — 37
PIZZA SOUP — 39
SOUTHWESTERN SWEET POTATO SOUP — 40
THAI COCONUT CURRY SOUP — 42

HOMEMADE CHICKEN BROTH

A pot full of simmering chicken broth is the essence of home cooking: true flavour brimming with hearty goodness, ready to launch a thousand other dishes. Try making a batch, dividing it into easily used amounts and keeping them in your freezer, ready for whatever idea comes along. You can use any chicken, but a stewing hen will have the most flavour. MAKES 3 TO 4 QUARTS (3 TO 4 L)

1 large chicken cut into parts
2 large onions (unpeeled),
  cut into eighths
2 carrots, cut into 1-inch (2.5 cm)
  chunks

2 stalks of celery, cut into 1-inch
  (2.5 cm) chunks
2 bay leaves
a sprig or two of fresh thyme

Freestyle VARIATION

For a deeper, richer flavour, try roasting the chicken parts first, at 350°F (180°C), until they are golden brown and caramelized. Be sure to dissolve any lingering golden bits in the roasting pan and add them to the simmering stock; they'll be full of concentrated flavour. It is possible to flavour a chicken broth with any number of leftover vegetables and fresh herbs, but it's not always a good idea. Because the broth is usually used as a flavour base for another dish, it's best to flavour it simply, to keep it neutral so it doesn't overpower the dish.

Toss everything into a large stockpot and cover with cold water. Begin heating over high heat. Almost bring the water to a boil, and then reduce the heat and maintain a gentle simmer. It's not necessary to cover the pot. As the broth begins to simmer the chicken will release various impurities and fat. These will foam and rise to the top. Skim them away so they don't cloud the broth, but don't worry if some stay behind. They won't affect the flavour.

Continue simmering for about 2 hours or so until the chicken is cooked through and the broth is flavourful.

Remove the chicken meat and reserve for another use.

Strain the broth and cool at room temperature for an hour or so before covering and refrigerating. As the broth cools in the refrigerator, any remaining fat will rise to the surface and harden, where it can be easily removed and discarded.

CHICKEN NOODLE SOUP

A bowl of homemade chicken noodle soup is one of the most comforting foods you can place on your table. It's a great way to show off the hearty goodness of homemade chicken broth. It's also a great way to show off your creativity by personalizing the flavour any way you care to. SERVES 4

a splash of vegetable oil
1 carrot, peeled and finely diced
1 stalk of celery, finely diced
1 onion, peeled and finely diced
2 or 3 cloves of garlic, thinly sliced
  (optional)
4 cups (1 L) of chicken broth (see page
  24 for homemade)

1 cup (250 mL) of shredded meat
  from the broth (optional)
1 cup (250 mL) of your favourite
  noodle or pasta
a handful of flat leaf parsley, chopped
a few sprigs of fresh thyme, stems
  removed, leaves minced
1 green onion, thinly sliced

Splash the vegetable oil into a stockpot, enough to cover the bottom in a thin film. Begin heating over medium-high heat. Add the vegetables and garlic and sauté them for a few minutes, heating them through and brightening their flavours.

Add the chicken broth and bring it to a simmer. Add the chicken meat, if using, and the noodles or pasta and continue cooking until the noodles are tender. Stir in the parsley, fresh thyme and green onion. Serve immediately.

You can add any vegetable or fresh herb you like to this soup. You can also use a favourite flavour theme like Mediterranean, stirring in zucchini, sun-dried tomatoes and a spoonful or two of Basil Pesto (page 246), or Southwestern, with tomatoes, bell peppers, chili peppers, chili powder, cumin and cilantro.

CREAM OF MUSHROOM SOUP

The earthy flavour of mushrooms shine through in this soup. This soup's rich hearty flavour will easily satisfy your mushroom craving, and there's enough for seconds or leftovers. It also shows off how well meaty mushrooms and red wine go together. SERVES 4 TO 6

1 stick (½ cup/125 mL) of butter
2 lb (1 kg) of button mushrooms,
  rinsed and sliced
3 onions, peeled and chopped
a sprinkle or two of sea salt
  and freshly ground pepper
½ bottle or so of any hearty red wine

4 cups (1 L) of chicken broth
  (see page 24 for homemade)
1 cup (250 mL) of heavy cream (35%)
1 tablespoon (15 mL) or more of
  chopped fresh thyme
2 tablespoons (30 mL) of cornstarch
¼ cup (60 mL) of water

Freestyle VARIATION

You may use any mushroom or combination of mushrooms to make this soup. Shiitakes in particular are an excellent choice because they add a rich meaty flavour. You may also finish the soup with any of your favourite herbs. Rosemary and tarragon are excellent choices. If you prefer a smoother texture, feel free to purée all, or part of, this soup.

Place a large stockpot over medium-high heat. Add the butter, mushrooms and onions. Season with salt and pepper. Sauté until lightly browned. The mushrooms will initially release a lot of moisture, preventing them from browning. Eventually that moisture will evaporate, allowing the pot's heat to rise to browning temperature.

Pour in the red wine and bring it to a simmer. Continue cooking—the moisture in the wine will evaporate, concentrating its flavour—until the wine has reduced by about two-thirds.

Add the chicken broth, heavy cream and fresh thyme. Stir well and bring the soup to a simmer.

Meanwhile, dissolve the cornstarch in the water. Add this mixture slowly to the simmering soup, stirring until it returns to the simmer and thickens slightly. If you prefer your soup a bit thicker, feel free to add more cornstarch. Taste and add more salt and pepper, if desired. Serve immediately.

FRENCH ONION SOUP

This soup is like culinary alchemy: creating gold from virtually nothing. It's amazing how much flavour you can coax out of an onion with patience. Taking the time to slowly brown an onion is one of the most satisfying things you can do in the kitchen. It's the key to the rich, deep flavour in a bowl of true onion soup. SERVES 4 TO 6

CARAMELIZED ONIONS
½ stick (¼ cup/60 mL) of butter
2 tablespoons (30 mL) of any
   vegetable oil
4 large onions, peeled and
   thinly sliced
a splash of water
a sprinkle or two of sea salt
   and freshly ground pepper

SOUP
½ cup (125 mL) of brandy, sherry,
   cognac or fortified wine such as
   Madeira or Marsala
4 cups (1 L) of chicken broth (see
   page 24 for homemade)
leaves from 2 sprigs of fresh thyme
a sprinkle or two of sea salt and freshly
   ground pepper
4 slices of hearty multi-grain bread
2 cups (500 mL) of shredded Swiss,
   Gruyère or Emmenthal cheese

For the caramelized onions, toss the butter and oil into a large heavy stockpot set over medium-high heat. Melt the butter—the oil will protect the butter and its flavour from burning—and then add the onions, a splash of water and salt and pepper. Stir well, then cover with a tight-fitting lid. This will capture steam and help the onions release all their moisture.

Cook, stirring now and then, until the onions soften and become quite wet, about 10 minutes. Remove the lid and continue cooking over medium-high heat, stirring frequently until all the water has evaporated. Lower the heat a bit and slowly begin to caramelize the onions, stirring them frequently. This will take about 1 hour. You don't need to stir continuously, just enough to keep the onions from sticking to the bottom. Continuing to lower the heat will also help prevent sticking.

For the soup, when the onions are a deep golden colour and have shrunk dramatically, add the brandy. Turn up the heat and cook for a few minutes, stirring constantly, until the additional liquid seems to have evaporated. Add the chicken broth and bring to a simmer. Add the thyme leaves, season with salt and pepper and continue cooking for 15 minutes or so.

To serve, preheat the broiler in your oven. Toast the bread slices to add flavour and help absorb the soup. Cut rounds out of the toast, large enough to fit your soup bowls.

Ladle the soup into 4 ovenproof serving bowls. Top each with a slice or two of toasted bread rounds, enough to cover the top of the soup. Cover the bread with an even mound of shredded cheese. Broil until the cheese has melted and browned and looks beautiful.

freestyle VARIATION

You may use any onion to make this soup, but your best choice is simply white cooking onions. Red onions cost more and eventually lose their colour. Try stirring some sliced green onions or chives into the soup just before you ladle it into the bowls.

LOUISIANA SHRIMP GUMBO

This classic soup is more than a meal in a bowl. It's a way to show off the bright spicy flavours of Louisiana and the distinctive cooking style that has made gumbo one of the world's great dishes. SERVES 4 TO 6

1 cup (250 mL) of any vegetable oil
1 cup (250 mL) of all-purpose flour
1 onion, peeled and chopped
1 green pepper, seeded
   and chopped
1 stalk of celery, chopped
4 cloves of garlic, peeled
2 cups (500 mL) of chicken broth
   (see page 24 for homemade)
6 oz (175 g) or so of andouille, chorizo
   or Italian sausage, sliced
8 oz (250 g) of shrimp, peeled
   and deveined

one 28 oz (796 mL) can
   of whole tomatoes
4 oz (125 g) of okra, fresh or frozen
1 teaspoon (5 mL) of paprika
1 teaspoon (5 mL) of onion powder
1 teaspoon (5 mL) of garlic powder
1 teaspoon (5 mL) of dried oregano
1 teaspoon (5 mL) of dried thyme
1 teaspoon (5 mL) of sassafras
   (gumbo filé powder)
¼ teaspoon (1 mL) of cayenne pepper
a sprinkle or two of sea salt
2 green onions, thinly sliced

Freestyle VARIATION

Louisiana cooking is heavily flavoured and often quite spicy, so add more of the spices if you like. Try stirring in any seafood during the last few minutes of cooking. You may also omit the shrimp and substitute a chicken cut into pieces and browned.

Preheat a large, heavy-bottomed stockpot over medium heat.

Pour in the vegetable oil and, when it's smoking hot, gradually and carefully whisk in the flour, forming a "roux." Continue stirring the roux, whisking constantly until it begins to deepen in colour. Be careful, it's very hot! This browning process weakens the roux's ability to thicken the gumbo, but it also adds lots of authentic, distinctive flavour.

After 5 minutes or so, when the roux is a deep golden brown, add the Holy Trinity of Louisiana cooking: the onion, green pepper and celery. Add the garlic cloves and stir them for a few minutes until they've softened. Add the chicken broth and stir until it thickens. Add the sausage, shrimp, tomatoes, okra, herbs and spices. Taste and season with salt.

Simmer until the sausages and shrimp are cooked through, about 10 minutes. Add the green onions. Serve immediately.

MARITIME CLAM CHOWDER

In the Maritimes we don't worry whether our chowders are authentic or not. We know a true clam chowder is just a bowl full of simple, hearty flavours. We often use canned clams and always stir in onions, potatoes and milk. We're too busy asking for seconds to worry whether we got it right! SERVES 4

4 slices of bacon, chopped
a splash of water
1 onion, peeled and chopped
2 stalks of celery, chopped
a generous splash of any white wine
1 cup (250 mL) of heavy cream (35%)
1 cup (250 mL) of milk
two 5 oz (142 g) cans of clam meat
1 large baking potato (unpeeled), coarsely grated

2 bay leaves
leaves from 3 or 4 sprigs of fresh thyme
one 12 oz (354 mL) can of unsweetened evaporated milk or 1⅓ cups (330 mL) of regular milk
a sprinkle or two of sea salt and freshly grated pepper
a handful of flat leaf parsley leaves

Freestyle VARIATION

For a distinctive flavour, try adding a spoonful or two of horseradish to the chowder. For a luxurious special-occasion treat, add lots of smoked salmon. You may also try stirring in one of your favourite fresh herbs at the last second. Dill and tarragon are traditional, as are green onions. You may also stir in chunks of any fish you like, even canned tuna fish.

Toss the bacon pieces into a thick-bottomed stockpot with a splash of water. By adding water to the raw bacon you're less likely to burn it as it gradually releases its fat and browns evenly.

Stir over medium-high heat until the bacon crisps nicely.

Pour off most of the fat. Add another splash of water to loosen the flavourful bits on the bottom and then add the onions and celery. Sauté them for a few minutes until they soften and smell great.

Add the white wine, cream, milk, clam meat, grated potato and the bay and thyme leaves. Bring the mixture to a slow simmer, stirring frequently. Turn the heat down a notch or two and continue simmering until the grated

} A baking potato is the best choice for thickening the chowder because its high-starch, low-moisture flesh dissolves so easily.

potato softens, releasing its starches and thickening the chowder, about 20 minutes.

Add the evaporated (or regular) milk and continue stirring until it's heated through. Taste the chowder and season it well with salt and pepper. Stir in the parsley and serve immediately. If you like, this chowder can be made a day or two in advance and then reheated. Its flavour actually gets better when it rests overnight.

MUSHROOM MISO BROTH WITH BUCKWHEAT NOODLES

You won't believe how richly satisfying a bowl of this broth can be and how easy it is to make. Miso is a fermented paste made from soybeans. It's very nutritious and a staple of Japanese and vegetarian cooking. If you can boil water, you can make this broth. SERVES 4

4 cups (1 L) of chicken broth (see
   page 24 for homemade) or water
a small knob of frozen ginger
2 cups (500 mL) of shiitake or button
   mushrooms, thinly sliced
8 oz (250 g) of Japanese soba
   (buckwheat) noodles

4 heaping tablespoons (60 mL)
   of fresh miso paste
a dash or two of hot pepper sauce
   to taste
1 sheet of nori seaweed, finely
   shredded with scissors
2 green onions, thinly sliced

Bring the chicken broth (or water) to a simmer in a stockpot.

Grate the frozen ginger into the broth with a Microplane grater or the smallest holes on a standard box grater. Add the mushrooms and continue cooking until tender, about 10 minutes or so.

Add the soba noodles and continue simmering until nearly tender, about 5 minutes. Stir in the miso paste, hot sauce, nori seaweed and green onions. Continue cooking just long enough to heat everything through, about 1 minute. Miso is a bit delicate so it's always best to add it to the hot liquid and then serve it immediately. Miso broth is fine if it sits a while but it tastes best freshly made.

freestyle VARIATION

Try adding a handful of bean sprouts or chopped Asian greens to the simmering broth. For an even richer flavour, feel free to add more miso paste. There are many types to choose from, ranging from light to dark. In general, the flavour gets stronger as the colour gets darker. Some are even flavoured with fermented grains.

PIZZA SOUP

You can easily fit the kid-friendly flavours of a pizza into a soup bowl. This easy-to-make soup is always a hit at our table. SERVES 4

2 tablespoons (30 mL) of olive oil
2 onions, peeled and chopped
4 cloves of garlic, minced
one 28 oz (796 mL) can of whole,
   crushed or chopped tomatoes
2 cups (500 mL) of chicken broth
   (see page 24 for homemade)
2 carrots, peeled and grated

1 tablespoon (15 mL) of dried oregano
8 oz (250 g) of pepperoni, thinly sliced
a sprinkle of sea salt and freshly
   ground black pepper
4 slices of whole grain bread
2 cups (500 mL) of shredded
   mozzarella cheese

Sauté the onions and garlic in a large stockpot with the olive oil until the onions are lightly browned and your kitchen smells amazing.

Add the canned tomatoes. (If you use whole tomatoes crush them with the back of a wooden spoon.) Add the chicken broth, carrots and oregano. Simmer for 15 minutes or so until the carrots are tender.

Add the pepperoni and season with salt and pepper to taste.

Preheat the broiler in your oven.

Ladle the hot soup into 4 onion soup bowls or 4 large ovenproof soup cups. Cut the bread into large circles and cover the top of each soup bowl. Sprinkle ½ cup (125 mL) of shredded mozzarella onto the top of each bread slice and then place bowls under the broiler in your oven. Cook until the cheese is golden and bubbling, about 2 or 3 minutes.

Try adding any of your favourite pizza toppings to the soup. Mushrooms, peppers and sliced, browned Italian sausage all work well.

SOUTHWESTERN SWEET POTATO SOUP

Sweet potatoes are packed with flavour and nutritional goodness. They're one of the healthiest ingredients in your kitchen. They also purée easily, smoothly thickening this brightly flavoured soup. SERVES 4 TO 6

¼ cup (60 mL) of any vegetable oil
2 large onions, peeled and chopped
4 cloves of garlic, sliced
4 cups (1 L) of chicken broth (see
    page 24 for homemade)
2 large sweet potatoes, washed,
    peeled and grated
1 chipotle pepper, packed
    in adobo sauce

1 teaspoon (5 mL) of ground cinnamon
1 teaspoon (5 mL) of ground cumin
a sprinkle or two of sea salt
½ cup (125 mL) of sour cream
1 bunch of cilantro, finely minced
1 whole wheat or soft corn tortilla
4 to 6 sprigs of fresh cilantro,
    for garnish

Freestyle VARIATION

You may use any chili pepper you like to add spicy flair to this soup. Chipotles are not too spicy and they add lots of smoky flavour. They're actually smoked jalapeños and can be bought dried or packed in adobo sauce, a traditional Mexican tomato sauce. Poblanos or ancho peppers are also excellent choices.

Preheat your oven to 375°F (190°C).

Place a large stockpot over medium-high heat and add the oil and onions. Sauté the onions until they're golden brown. Add the garlic and continue cooking for a few minutes more. Garlic burns much faster than onions, so adding it later keeps that from happening.

Pour in the broth and stir in the grated sweet potatoes. Bring to a simmer and then add the chipotle pepper, cinnamon, cumin and salt. Continue simmering until the sweet potatoes soften.

Carefully purée using a blender, food processor or immersion blender. Taste and add a bit more salt if you like. You may also thin the soup by adding 1 cup (250 mL) or so more of water or broth.

As the soup simmers get the garnishes ready. Stir the cilantro into the sour cream. Roll the tortilla into a thick cigar shape, slice thinly and place on a baking sheet and bake until crispy, about 15 minutes.

Ladle the soup into festive soup bowls, top with a dollop of cilantro sour cream, sprinkle on some crisp tortilla chips and top with a sprig of cilantro for garnish.

THAI COCONUT CURRY SOUP

The sweet, sour, spicy, salty and savoury flavours of Thailand are one of my favourite ways to fill a bowl. They're seductively addictive, always well balanced and help define one of the world's great cuisines. They're also easy! This is a very simple dish to make. SERVES 4

two 14 oz (398 mL) cans of premium
    coconut milk
1 heaping tablespoon (15 mL) of Thai
    curry paste
roots of 1 bunch of cilantro, rinsed well
    (see Variation, page 74)
2 boneless, skinless chicken breasts,
    thinly sliced
2 cups (500 mL) of chicken broth
    (see page 24 for homemade)
1 carrot, shredded
4 or 5 lime leaves

2 stalks of lemon grass, halved length-
    wise, woody leaves removed
2 tablespoons (30 mL) of fish sauce
zest and juice of 2 limes
a small knob of frozen ginger
a handful of bean sprouts
one 8 oz (225 g) package
    of rice noodles
leaves of 1 bunch of cilantro,
    rinsed well
2 or 3 green onions, thinly sliced
a sprinkle or two of salt or soy sauce

Freestyle VARIATION

Thai curry pastes get their heat from chili peppers, but they're also loaded with other flavours. You may use as much or as little as you like. Yellow is the mildest; green the hottest. Try stirring in a head of chopped Asian greens or baby spinach with the bean sprouts. You may easily substitute beef or shrimp for the chicken.

Scoop the thick coconut cream from the top of just one of the cans into a large stockpot set over a medium-high heat. Melt the cream, add the curry paste and stir for a few minutes until they begin to sizzle.

Add the cilantro roots and chicken and sauté until the chicken is cooked through, about 5 minutes.

Add the coconut milk from the first can and all the contents of the second can along with the chicken broth, carrot, lime leaves, lemon grass, fish sauce and lime zest and juice. Grate the frozen ginger into the broth with a Microplane grater or standard box grater. Simmer for 20 minutes or so.

Stir in the bean sprouts. Add the rice noodles, gently pushing them beneath the surface of the broth. Turn off the heat and let stand until the noodles soften, about 5 minutes. Rice noodles don't need to simmer like pasta to cook; they simply need to rehydrate in the hot liquid.

Stir in most of the cilantro leaves. Remove the lemon grass stalks. Taste and season with a touch more salt (or soy sauce) as needed. Ladle into large bowls and garnish with the green onions and remaining cilantro leaves.

SALADS

ASIAN CUCUMBER MINT SALAD

This is a salad of contrast and balance. The sweetness of the cucumbers is sharpened by the sourness of the spicy dressing, which in turn is cooled by the refreshing mint. SERVES 4

1 large cucumber, sliced as thinly
   as possible
1 red onion, thinly sliced
1 carrot, grated
a handful of mint leaves
zest and juice of 1 lemon

1 tablespoon (15 mL) of olive oil
1 tablespoon (15 mL) of honey
1 teaspoon (5 mL) of soy sauce
½ teaspoon (2 mL) of sriracha, or your
   favourite hot sauce

I often toss bean sprouts into this salad. Salted peanuts sprinkled in at the last moment are an excellent addition as well. If you're a fan of Thai flavours, add a splash of fish sauce.

In a large salad bowl toss together the cucumber, onion, carrot, mint, lemon zest and juice, olive oil, honey, soy sauce and hot sauce until well combined. Serve immediately or let it rest for a few hours. The texture will change as the acidic lemon juice and honey in the dressing draw moisture out of the cucumber. The salad will get a bit watery and soften. That's okay; it still tastes great. Just toss again before serving.

CAESAR SALAD WITH BASIL

This classic salad has come a long way since its 1924 invention by Caesar Cardini at his Tijuana restaurant. It's now found on virtually every menu in the country—at home and in restaurants. Because there are as many ways to make it as there are cooks, I don't spend a lot of time worrying about authenticity, just flavour. My version includes the wonderfully aromatic addition of whole basil leaves. SERVES 4 TO 6

½ loaf of Italian bread
a few generous splashes of olive oil
2 heads of romaine lettuce
a handful or two of whole basil leaves
1 red onion, thinly sliced

½ cup (125 mL) of Caesar Dressing
    (see page 63)
a sprinkle or two of sea salt and freshly
    ground pepper

Freestyle VARIATION

Try adding some crumbled bacon to the salad or, for a more elegant garnish, using a vegetable peeler to shave long slices from a wedge of Parmesan cheese. You may also leave the romaine leaves whole; that's how Caesar Cardini originally did it. For a unique flavour boost, cut the whole lettuce head in half lengthwise and grill it. You can also top any version with grilled chicken or shrimp to elevate the salad into a meal.

Preheat your oven to 350°F (180°C).

Cut the bread into cubes and toss with enough olive oil to lightly coat each one. Spread the cubes in a single layer on a baking sheet and bake until golden brown and crisp, about 15 minutes.

Meanwhile, tear the lettuce into bite-sized pieces and toss it with the basil leaves, red onion and ½ cup (125 mL) or so of Caesar Dressing. Sprinkle the croutons on top and season with salt and pepper.

GRILLED PINEAPPLE RED ONION SALAD

This is my all-time favourite summer salad. It's amazing how much savoury flavour your grill can add to a simple pineapple and some red onion. Next time you fire up the works, try this salad and you'll have a new favourite for your repertoire too! SERVES 4

1 whole pineapple, skinned (uncored),
   cut into thick rings
2 red onions, sliced into a few very
   thick rings
a few generous splashes of olive oil

a sprinkle or two of sea salt and freshly
   ground pepper
zest and juice of 1 lemon
a few handfuls or more of fresh whole
   basil leaves

Preheat your barbecue or grill.

Evenly brush or drizzle the pineapple and onion rings with olive oil and season to taste with salt and pepper. Try to keep the onion rings intact as you do.

Grill the pineapple until golden grill marks appear and the fruit softens, about 5 minutes per side. Meanwhile, grill the onion until soft and lightly charred.

Quarter the grilled pineapple slices into wedges and roughly chop the onion rings. Toss everything with the lemon zest and juice and as many whole basil leaves as you can get your hands on.

This salad is very good tossed with a grilled chicken breast or two. Try tossing in some shredded coconut or sliced green onions as well.

LEMON FENNEL SLAW

This salad really shows off why fennel is one of my favourite vegetables. It's loaded with crisp sweetness and subtle licorice flavours. Try it. Its simplicity will blow you away! It'll soon be one of your favourites too. SERVES 2 TO 4

1 fennel bulb
zest and juice of ½ lemon
1 tablespoon (15 mL) of honey

a few splashes of olive oil
a sprinkle or two of sea salt and freshly
  ground pepper

Remove the stalks from the top of the fennel bulb. Cut the head in half through the core. Carefully trim out the woody core and then slice the remaining bulb as thinly as possible. Alternatively, shred it through the large holes of a box grater.

Specialty kitchen stores sell a fancy French slicing tool known as a mandoline which the pros use to slice fennel, onions and potatoes paper thin. It's nice to have one, but if you don't—no worries—the salad still tastes awesome made with grated fennel.

Whisk the lemon zest and juice, honey, olive oil and salt and pepper together in a nice salad bowl. Toss with the fennel and then grab some forks!

freestyle VARIATION

For lots of fresh herb flavour, toss a handful of cool mint leaves, sharply sliced chives or aromatic basil leaves into the salad. You can also toss in the feathery fronds from the top of the fennel. This salad may be made well in advance and tossed again at the last second. Its texture will soften a bit but it will still be bright and vibrant.

ROASTED POTATO BACON SALAD

One of the best ways to add flavour to any ingredient is to roast it, especially the humble potato. That simple twist elevates this classic salad into something memorable. Add in the sharp flavours of capers, mustard and vinegar, and you'll have a new family classic. SERVES 4

4 or 5 thick slices of bacon
20 or so baby red potatoes
a sprinkle or two of sea salt and freshly
 ground pepper
a handful of flat leaf parsley leaves

a few pickles, diced small
1 tablespoon (15 mL) of grainy mustard
1 tablespoon (15 mL) of mayonnaise
a splash of red wine vinegar

By adding water to the raw bacon, you're less likely to burn it as it gradually releases its fat and browns evenly. When the water evaporates and the bacon begins to brown, turn the heat down a notch and continue cooking until it's all nice and crisp.

Stack the bacon slices on top of each other, then cut them into thin pieces. Toss them into a large sauté pan, add a splash of water and begin heating the works over medium-high heat. Strain and reserve the fat. Set aside the bacon.

Meanwhile, preheat your oven to 400°F (200°C).

Cut the baby potatoes in half. Toss them with the bacon fat and salt and pepper and roast them until they're golden brown, about 40 minutes. Cool to room temperature.

Toss the potatoes with the bacon pieces, parsley, pickles, mustard, mayonnaise and vinegar, then serve right away or save for later. This salad is great when it's made the night before a party.

For a special-occasion twist, try using capers instead of pickles, or you can skip the pickles and use a few spoonfuls of pickled green relish instead. You can also try using a big handful of fresh dill fronds along with the parsley leaves. While baby red potatoes are my favourite, you may also use any other type of potato to make this salad.

SOUTHWESTERN BEAN SALAD

Bean salads are excellent stick-to-the-ribs fare, especially when they're jazzed up with the bright flavours of the Southwest, where beans have long been a staple food. SERVES 4 TO 6

½ cup (125 mL) of olive oil
¼ cup (60 mL) of red wine vinegar
1 tablespoon (15 mL) of Dijon mustard
½ teaspoon (2 mL) or more of your
  favourite hot sauce
one 14 oz (398 mL) can of mixed
  beans, drained and rinsed well
1 cup (250 mL) of cooked corn or raw
  corn sliced off the cob
1 red bell pepper, diced small

1 basket of cherry tomatoes, halved
1 red onion, thinly sliced
a handful of green beans, steamed and
  cut into bite-sized pieces
a handful of yellow wax beans,
  steamed and cut into bite-sized
  pieces
a bunch of fresh cilantro, minced
a sprinkle or two of sea salt and freshly
  ground pepper

In a festive salad bowl, whisk together the oil, vinegar, mustard and hot sauce. Add the mixed beans, corn, bell pepper, tomatoes, red onion, green beans, wax beans, cilantro and salt and pepper, and toss to combine. Season to taste. Serve immediately or rest for a few hours.

This salad is excellent with a grilled chicken breast or two sliced into it. You may also take the time to grill the bell pepper, corn and red onion. For lots of spicy Southwestern flavour, try adding a minced fresh jalapeño or chipotle pepper packed in adobo sauce.

SESAME SPINACH SALAD

This is one of Rachel's specialties; she makes it all the time and can whip it up in seconds. It's one of my favourites because its flavours are exotic yet still very familiar and comforting. SERVES 4

½ teaspoon (2 mL) of sesame oil
1 tablespoon (15 mL) of tahini
   (sesame paste)
1 teaspoon (5 mL) of soy sauce
zest and juice of 1 lemon
4 handfuls of baby spinach leaves

1 handful of bean sprouts
1 small red onion, thinly sliced
1 tablespoon (15 mL) of sesame seeds
a few sheets of nori seaweed,
   thinly sliced

In the bottom of a festive salad bowl whisk together the sesame oil, tahini, soy sauce and lemon zest and juice. Toss with the spinach leaves, bean sprouts, red onion, sesame seeds, and the sliced nori.

For an even more Asian flavour, try adding a handful of cilantro leaves with the spinach leaves. For a different version, try wilting the spinach, red onion and bean sprouts with the sesame oil and soy sauce before tossing them with all the other ingredients.

STRAWBERRY ARUGULA SALAD

This salad features one of my all-time favourite flavour combinations: peppery, nutty arugula leaves tossed with sweet, fragrant strawberries, mellow balsamic, aromatic fennel seed and sweet pine nuts. Together these ingredients are far more than the sum of their parts. SERVES 4

4 handfuls of arugula
2 cups (500 mL) of sliced local
    strawberries

½ cup (125 mL) of pine nuts
¼ cup (60 mL) of Fennel Balsamic
    Dressing (see page 63)

Simply toss the arugula, strawberries, pine nuts and dressing together until well combined. That's it—it's that simple!

Try adding some segmented orange sections or substituting sliced almonds for the pine nuts.

TEN SALAD DRESSINGS

It's easy to make your own personalized salad dressings. The basic ratio of sour, sweet and oil is easily modified and infinitely variable. This recipe makes enough for several salads because it's just as easy to make a lot as a little and, once you taste your own dressings, you won't be able to get enough. MAKES ABOUT 2 CUPS (500 ML)

MASTER RECIPE

1 cup (250 mL) of extra virgin olive oil

½ cup (125 mL) of any vinegar, lemon or lime juice

½ cup (125 mL) of honey, maple syrup, or jelly

1 heaping tablespoon (15 mL) of Dijon mustard

1 heaping tablespoon (15 mL) of any fresh herb or spice (optional)

a sprinkle or two of sea salt and freshly ground pepper

Simply decide which ingredients you'd like to use and then measure everything into a Mason jar and shake vigorously until combined. Your personalized dressing will stay fresh in your refrigerator for several weeks, if it lasts that long.

Freestyle VARIATIONS

1. **SHERRY MAPLE** Sherry vinegar and maple syrup

2. **FENNEL BALSAMIC** Balsamic vinegar, honey and ground fennel seed

3. **RASPBERRY** Red wine vinegar and raspberry jelly

4. **ITALIAN** Red wine vinegar, no sweetener, minced garlic, oregano and thyme

5. **CAESAR** Lemon juice, no sweetener, ½ cup (125 mL) of Parmesan cheese, 1 tablespoon (15 mL) of minced garlic, 1 tablespoon (15 mL) of Worcestershire sauce

6. **CARIBBEAN** Lime zest and juice, honey and shredded coconut

7. **SOUTHWESTERN** Lime zest and juice, honey, cilantro and hot sauce

8. **VANILLA** White wine vinegar, honey and pure vanilla extract

9. **GOAT CHEESE** 1 small 5 oz (150 g) log of goat cheese, ¼ cup (60 mL) of white wine vinegar, ½ cup (125 mL) of olive oil, 1 tablespoon (15 mL) of honey, and a sprinkle or two of salt and pepper, puréed smooth

10. **TOMATO** 1 large ripe local tomato puréed with the zest and juice of 2 lemons and ½ cup (125 mL) of olive oil, seasoned with salt and pepper

TWENTY-FRUIT FRUIT SALAD

This is one of Gabe's favourite snacks. He loves fruit so we play around in the kitchen and see how many different kinds of citrus fruit, melons, tree fruit, grapes, berries and tropical fruit we can toss into one salad bowl. Our record is 32! MAKES ENOUGH FOR A CROWD, OR FOR SEVERAL DAYS OF SNACKING

orange, skinned and segmented	green grapes
grapefruit, skinned and segmented	black grapes
cantaloupe, skinned	strawberries
watermelon, skinned	raspberries
honeydew, skinned	blueberries
apples, diced	mangoes, skinned and diced
peaches, diced	pineapple, skinned and diced
pears, diced	kiwis, skinned and diced
plums, diced	papaya, skinned and diced
apricots, diced	zest and juice of 2 limes
red grapes	a spoonful or two of honey

Prepare all the fruit you can find, removing any unnecessary skin or seeds. Make sure all the fruit is in bite-sized chunks, and toss together with the lime zest and juice and the honey. You may serve this salad immediately but, if you refrigerate it for a few hours, it will become even juicier and more delicious.

This will keep in the fridge for 2 to 3 days.

Next time you're at the supermarket, load your cart with every different fruit you can find. They're all fair game in this salad.

BEEF

BLUE CHEESE-CRUSTED FILET MIGNON

Filet mignon is prized for its extreme tenderness, not for its rather bland flavour. It doesn't have the rich beefy flavour of a well-marbled steak, but it's still a rare treat and a great way to show off your kitchen's best, especially when you add lots of flavour with an easy-to-make blue cheese crust. SERVES 4

4 filet mignon steaks
a sprinkle or two of sea salt and freshly
   ground pepper
a splash or two any vegetable oil
6 oz (175 g) of blue cheese

2 slices of whole grain bread, cubed
½ stick (¼ cup/60 mL) of butter
2 sprigs of fresh rosemary, thyme
   or tarragon
more freshly ground pepper

Preheat your oven to 400°F (200°C). Preheat a large heavy skillet over medium-high heat.

Season the filets well and rub them with vegetable oil. Carefully position them in the hot pan and sear for a minute or so on each side, leaving the interiors raw and cool. Because the meat will be protected by a crust and will finish cooking in a relatively cool oven, this is your only chance to add caramelized flavour to the meat. Place steaks on a cooling rack set over a baking sheet.

Purée the blue cheese, bread, butter, fresh herbs and pepper in a food processor until smooth. Pack the blue cheese crust mixture onto the tops of the filets, evenly covering each one with a thick layer of flavour. Bake the crusted filets in the oven until medium-rare, about 15 minutes. To be sure, insert a meat thermometer into the centre of each filet. When the temperature reads 135°F to 140°F (57°C to 60°C), they're done.

You can prepare the crusted filets in advance and refrigerate them until you are ready to roast them. If you do, add a few minutes more to the roasting time. You may also substitute aged cheddar cheese for the blue cheese.

FIRE-GRILLED STEAK
WITH STEAKHOUSE BUTTER

The only thing better than a fire-grilled steak is the same steak with a round of flavoured butter slowly melting overtop, forming a rich, tasty sauce as it mingles with the steak's juices. For the ultimate grilled steak experience, try taking the time to build a hardwood fire in your backyard! SERVES 4

STEAKHOUSE BUTTER
1 stick (½ cup/125 mL) of butter, softened
2 tablespoons (30 mL) of finely minced shallot or red onion
1 clove of garlic, finely minced
1 tablespoon (15 mL) of finely minced parsley
1 tablespoon (15 mL) of finely minced fresh thyme

2 tablespoons (30 mL) of red wine vinegar
a sprinkle or two of sea salt and freshly ground pepper

STEAK
4 thick New York striploins, sirloins or rib-eye steaks
a sprinkle or two of sea salt and freshly ground pepper for each steak

Try rubbing the each steak with a halved garlic clove before you season and grill.

For the steakhouse butter, stir the butter, shallot or onion, garlic, parsley, thyme, vinegar and salt and pepper together until thoroughly combined.

Place a piece of plastic wrap on your work surface. Scoop the butter along the edge, forming a log shape roughly 4 inches (10 cm) long. Roll the butter once so it is nearly covered in the plastic wrap, then gently roll further. Tightly roll up the plastic wrap, grasp the ends of the plastic and twirl the works a few times, tightening the butter into a perfect round log.

Refrigerate or freeze for several hours or overnight until the butter is firm enough to slice.

For the steaks, build a hardwood fire and let it burn down to a thick bed of glowing hot coals, or preheat your grill to its highest setting. Just before you begin to cook the steaks, pat them dry and season them heavily with salt and pepper.

You may press steaks with your finger to gauge doneness; they stiffen as they cook through. This will take some time to master but it's a skill worth cultivating. You can also do what every novice professional cook does when the chef isn't looking: cut a small slice in the centre and have a peek!

Position them on the grill at a 45-degree angle to the grill grates. After a few minutes turn them 90 degrees to get the perfect steakhouse grill marks. Flip and repeat. Continue cooking until the steaks reach the doneness you prefer. Serve each steak with a thick slice of steakhouse butter on top.

OLD-FASHIONED BEEF STEW

Braising is my favourite cooking method. I just love the way it can transform an inexpensive, tough cut of beef into a tasty tender stew. Toss in the earthy flavours of root vegetables and aromatic red wine, and you are well on your way to a rich flavour base. But the real secret to a truly memorable beef stew is patiently browning the meat. SERVES 4 TO 6

2 lb (1 kg) of stewing beef
a sprinkle or two of sea salt and freshly
   ground pepper
a splash of any vegetable oil
a few carrots, peeled and roughly
   chopped
a few stalks of celery, roughly chopped
a few potatoes, peeled and
   roughly chopped
a few parsnips, peeled and
   roughly chopped
a few onions, peeled and
   roughly chopped

1 turnip, peeled and roughly chopped
one 28 oz (796 mL) can of whole
   tomatoes
½ bottle or so of hearty red wine
3 to 4 cups (750 mL to 1 L) of homemade or canned beef broth
a few bay leaves
a few sprigs of fresh rosemary
1 jar of pickled baby white onions
a few handfuls of frozen peas
another sprinkle or two of salt
   and pepper

Freestyle VARIATION

You may use any combination of root vegetables you have on hand. You may use any cut of beef that's labelled for stewing, simmering or braising. Try using fresh thyme instead of rosemary. You can also stir in several sliced green onions at the last second for a burst of colour and flavour. Shredded aged cheddar cheese or tangy blue cheeses are a great topping for each bowl.

Preheat a large thick-bottomed pot over medium-high heat.

Meanwhile, pat the beef dry with a clean towel and then cut it into large cubes and season it with the salt and pepper.

Add a splash of oil to the pot—enough to cover the bottom in a thin layer—and toss in enough meat to form a single sizzling layer. Sear the meat on every side until it's evenly browned.

> Be patient when you're browning the meat; it takes a little time but it's worth every minute. The caramelized flavours are the secret to a rich hearty stew. As the meat browns, remove it from the pan, adding more oil and meat as needed.

Once the meat is done, discard the remaining oil but keep all the browned bits in the pan; they'll add lots of flavour to the stew.

Add half of the vegetables—reserving the other half—and all the meat back to the pot. Add the tomatoes and enough wine and beef broth to barely cover the works. Add the bay leaves and rosemary and bring the pot to a simmer.

Continue cooking until the meat is almost tender, about 1 hour, then add the remaining vegetables and the baby onions. Adding the vegetables in 2 batches allows the first batch to dissolve into the stew while the second retains its shape, colour and texture. Continue simmering until the meat and veggies are tender, another 30 minutes or so. When the stew is tender, add the frozen peas and cook until heated through. Taste it and season as you like with salt and pepper.

ORANGE GINGER BEEF

Beef stews are a part of cooking all over the world. Cooks everywhere know they can simmer tough, inexpensive cuts of meat in a flavourful liquid and then fill their bowls with a rich tender stew. My family loves this "Asian" version ladled over spinach leaves and bean sprouts. It's a stew and a salad in the same bowl! SERVES 4

a splash of vegetable oil
1 lb (500 g) or so of stewing beef, cubed
a sprinkle or two of salt and pepper
2 onions, peeled and chopped
a small knob unpeeled ginger, thinly sliced
one 10 oz (284 mL) can of beef broth
1 cup (250 mL) of orange juice
1 cup (250 mL) of orange marmalade

a generous splash of soy sauce
1 tablespoon (15 mL) of five-spice powder
another sprinkle or two of salt and pepper
one 10 oz (300 g) bag of baby spinach
a handful of bean sprouts
1 bunch of green onions, chopped
a handful of cilantro leaves

Freestyle VARIATION

Cilantro roots have lots of flavour. If some are still attached to your bunch, rinse them well, chop them finely and stir them in while the stew simmers. They're loaded with cilantro flavour and can handle more heat than the delicate leaves. For some bright spicy Thai flavour, use 1 tablespoon (15 mL) of Thai curry paste instead of the Chinese five-spice powder.

Preheat a large pot over a medium-high heat and then splash in enough oil to thinly coat the bottom. Season, then sear the meat until it's evenly browned on all sides. Searing the meat first adds lots of rich caramelized flavours before adding the liquids that lower the pot's temperature to below what's needed to brown. Remove the meat and set aside for a moment.

Add the onions and ginger and stir for a few minutes until they are lightly browned. If the pan starts to burn, add a splash of water and continue.

> Ginger doesn't always have to be peeled, just rinsed. The flesh doesn't always have to be grated either—when it simmers it tenderizes nicely.

Return the meat to the pot and add the beef broth, orange juice, marmalade, soy sauce and five-spice powder. Bring the works to a simmer and then reduce the heat to the lowest setting that will maintain the simmer. Place a tight-fitting lid on the pot to contain the tenderizing steam. Continue simmering until the meat is tender enough to break into smaller pieces, about 1 hour. Taste and season the broth.

Divide the spinach and bean sprouts evenly among 4 bowls. Stir the green onions and cilantro leaves into the stew—reserving a few—and ladle over the veggies. Top with a sprinkling of the reserved cilantro leaves and enjoy!

PAN-ROASTED STEAK
WITH BROWNED ONIONS

You don't need a fire blazing in the backyard or a fancy barbecue to cook a great steak. Pan-roasting works well too, especially if you start with a great steak, use lots of butter and finish with browned onions. SERVES 2

2 thickly cut New York striploins,
    sirloins or rib-eye steaks
2 tablespoons (30 mL) of any
    vegetable oil
2 tablespoons (30 mL) of butter
a sprinkle or two of sea salt and
    freshly ground pepper

1 large (or 2 small) white onion,
    thinly sliced
2 or more cloves of garlic,
    finely minced
1 tablespoon (15 mL) of minced fresh
    thyme, tarragon or rosemary

Pat the steaks dry and season them well with salt and pepper.

Pour the oil into your heaviest skillet. Add the butter to the centre of the oil and begin melting over medium-high heat. Continue until the mixture foams. Because butter burns at a fairly low temperature, the oil, which burns at a much higher temperature, will dilute it a bit, keep it from burning and allow you to cook the steak in the flavourful butter.

Add the steaks to the pan and begin searing their first sides until they're crusty and caramelized, about 8 to 10 minutes. Adjust the heat as needed to keep the steaks sizzling. Flip the steaks and cook the other sides for another 6 to 8 minutes for medium-rare. Remove the steaks from the pan and rest on a cooling rack for a few minutes, covered with a piece of foil, to allow them to re-absorb their juices.

Add the onions and garlic to the pan and sauté for a few minutes until they become golden brown and caramelized. They will absorb the butter and any stray cooking juices from the steak. Season with salt and pepper. Toss in the fresh herbs and serve immediately, topping each steak with a generous spoonful of the onions.

To judge whether the steak is done, poke it with your finger; it will firm up as it cooks through. This skill takes some time to master, but it's a good one to have in your repertoire. You may also do what every novice line cook does when the chef isn't looking: cut a small slit in 1 side and peek at the centre.

Freestyle VARIATION

Once the onions have browned, try adding a splash of brandy or sherry to them. A spoonful of grainy mustard is also a great flavour boost for the onions. For added richness, try a splash of heavy cream or sour cream.

RED WINE–BRAISED SHORT RIBS

Short ribs are my favourite type of beef. No other cut has their rich beefiness and melt-in-your-mouth texture. Of course they do have to be slowly braised to release all that rich goodness, but that's just more time to anticipate the treat to come! SERVES 4

a few splashes of any vegetable oil
16 or so beef short ribs, each about
    2 to 3 inches (5 to 8 cm) long
4 onions, peeled and chopped
2 stalks of celery, chopped
2 large carrots, peeled and chopped
1 whole head of garlic cloves, peeled

a full bottle of big, beefy red wine
    (such as Cabernet Sauvignon,
    Shiraz / Syrah, Zinfandel)
a bunch of fresh rosemary
a few bay leaves
a sprinkle or two of sea salt and freshly
    ground pepper

Preheat your oven to 300°F (150°C).

Heat a large heavy skillet over medium-high heat and splash in enough oil to cover the bottom with a light film. Add the ribs in a single layer and brown, caramelizing them well on all sides.

Place the browned ribs on a platter, drain most of the fat from the pan and place it back over the heat.

Add the onions, celery, carrot and garlic to the hot pan and sauté for a few minutes until they heat through and smell great. Return the ribs to pan and cover with wine. Add the rosemary and bay leaves and season well with salt and pepper.

Cover with a tight-fitting lid or with tightly sealed foil, and place in the oven to braise for about 2 hours. The ribs are done when they're fork-tender and nearly falling off the bone.

Serve with your favourite mashed potatoes and the braising liquid.

As mentioned in an earlier braising recipe, be patient when you're browning the meat; it takes a little time but it's worth every minute. The caramelized flavours are the secret to a rich hearty braise. Because the majority of the ribs' cooking time happens slowly while the beef is submerged in liquid, browning the meat is the only chance you have to add the deep rich flavours of caramelization.

For an extra-special presentation, you can ask your butcher to leave the ribs whole. They're trickier to brown, but the results are worth it. You can skip the red wine and use beef broth instead. If you like, you can easily thicken the braising liquid into a sauce with 1 tablespoon (15 mL) or so of cornstarch. Try stirring some grainy mustard or horseradish into the braising liquid just before serving the ribs.

ROASTED PRIME RIB
WITH HORSERADISH SAUCE

Nothing gets your guests' attention at the table, or your attention in the kitchen, like spending nearly a hundred dollars on a piece of meat, but a prime rib doesn't have to be intimidating. Instead, impress yourself in your own kitchen by cooking it the way the pros do: with a two-step heating process and a few more dollars invested in an accurate meat thermometer. SERVES 8 TO 10

one 3- or 4-bone standing prime rib
   roast, about 7 lb (3.2 kg)
lots of sea salt and freshly
   ground pepper
1 cup (250 mL) of sour cream

½ cup (125 mL) of prepared
   horseradish
2 tablespoons (30 mL) or so of thinly
   sliced fresh chives

Place a roasting pan in the lower third of the oven and preheat it to 450°F (230°C).

Thoroughly dry the meat by patting it with paper towels. This will help it brown quickly by getting rid of any surface moisture. Rub the surface of the meat with lots of coarse sea salt and freshly ground black pepper.

To sear the top surface, place the roast—rib side up—in a roasting pan and roast for 30 minutes. Flip the roast over and turn the oven down to 300°F (150°C). Continue roasting until an instant-read thermometer placed in the thickest part of the meat reads 135°F to 140°F (57°C to 60°C), about 3 hours in total. This will give you a perfect medium-rare-to-medium roast. For medium, wait until the thermometer reads 150°F (65°C), about 30 minutes more.

Remove the roast from the oven and rest it in a warm place loosely covered with several layers of foil for 15 to 20 minutes. Its stressed-out fibres will relax and re-absorb the juices that concentrate under great pressure in the centre of the meat during roasting. The internal temperature will slowly rise another 5°F to 10°F (20°C to 23°C) or so. This is known as carryover cooking and is factored into the doneness judgment above.

Meanwhile, whisk together the sour cream, horseradish and chives. Once the meat has rested, slice away. Serve with the horseradish sauce.

Ask your butcher for a roast from the "small" end of the larger full prime rib; the end nearest the loin is prized for its full shape and tender flavour. Be sure to specify that the "chine" bone be removed; it's part of the backbone and will give you trouble slicing the meat. If the roast is "tied," it will roast more evenly, but it's not absolutely critical.

Roasting large cuts of meat requires a balance of cooking methods. A high-heat roast will yield the beautiful crisp outside that makes prime rib so tasty. But, by the time the inside cooks through, the high heat will lead to a burnt exterior. The high heat also stresses the meat, shrinking it and squeezing out the vital moisture. A low-heat roast, while slower to cook, will result in much less shrinkage and a more even doneness. Unfortunately, slow heat won't brown the outside as nicely as high, fast heat. The solution? A combination.

SOUTHWESTERN BEEF STEW

Long ago, the cooks of the world discovered the efficiency of simmering tough meat in tenderizing water. They also discovered that they could add lots of local flavour to make the results more interesting. Today, beef stews are a part of cuisines and cultures around the globe. This one features the bright familiar flavours of the Southwest. SERVES 4 TO 6

a few splashes of any vegetable oil
2 lb (1 kg) or so of stewing beef, cut
    into cubes
4 onions, peeled and thinly sliced
1 whole head of garlic cloves, peeled
2 red bell peppers, seeded and cut into
    1-inch chunks
1 or 2 jalapeño peppers, seeded
    and minced

2 tablespoons (30 mL) of chili powder
one 28 oz (796 mL) can of whole
    tomatoes
one 14 oz (398 mL) can of pinto, red or
    black beans, drained and rinsed
1 cup (250 mL) of frozen corn
1 bunch of cilantro, chopped

Thoroughly dry the beef by patting it with paper towels; dry beef will sear better.

Preheat a large heavy pot over medium-high heat and add enough oil to cover the bottom of the pot. A thin film is not enough. Add a single layer of the beef cubes. Brown evenly, adjusting the heat as needed to keep the meat sizzling. Medium-high heat usually works best. Be patient, this is the only chance you'll have to add the rich deep flavour of caramelization to the moist stew.

Rest the browned beef on a plate. Continue with the rest of the beef, browning it in batches. Add more oil as needed. Remove the meat and set aside.

Add the onions and garlic to the empty hot pan and stir well with a wooden spoon, scraping any brown bits from the bottom of the pan. Continue until the onions are golden brown. Add the red and jalapeño peppers. Stir in the chili powder, canned tomatoes, beans and the browned beef.

Stir well and bring to a simmer. Cover with a tight-fitting lid and continue at a low simmer over low heat for an hour or so.

When you are ready to serve, stir in the frozen corn and cilantro.

Freestyle VARIATION

For an extra layer of flavour, try grilling the meat first before simmering it. You may also top each serving with shredded cheddar cheese or sour cream.

THE PERFECT BURGER

The humble hamburger can easily be elevated to the heights of cuisine classics with the same attention to detail that any dish deserves. It can also be infinitely varied with lots of your personalized flavours. Ground chuck is your best choice because it has a higher fat content than ground round or ground sirloin.

SERVES 4

1½ lb (750 g) of ground chuck
1 small white onion, finely minced
1 tablespoon (15 mL) of soy sauce
1 tablespoon (15 mL) of Worcester-
    shire sauce

a sprinkle or two of freshly
    ground pepper
4 soft hamburger rolls

After you flip the burgers add a few pieces of crisp bacon and thinly sliced cheddar cheese to each one. For a pizza burger twist, add a spoonful of pizza sauce and some shredded mozzarella cheese. Sautéed mushrooms and blue cheese are also great. There are also many masterpieces to be built with lettuce, tomato, thinly sliced red onion, other cheeses, ketchup, mustard, BBQ sauce and your other favourite toppings.

Preheat your barbecue on its highest setting.

Toss the beef into a small mixing bowl. Add the onion and season with the soy sauce, Worcestershire sauce and pepper. Gently toss everything together until well combined.

Form into 4 evenly shaped burgers no more than 1 inch (2.5 cm) thick. Form a shallow hollow with your fingers in the centre of each burger. This will help each burger cook evenly, and the hollow will eventually disappear as the meat cooks through.

Cook for about 4 minutes per side. Resist the urge to press on the burgers with your spatula; this just encourages them to release valuable moisture and flavour. Flip and continue cooking until the burger is cooked through to your liking.

TUSCAN STEAK SALAD

In many Italian restaurants the menu term "Tuscan Beef" refers to a particular style of serving beef that is always dramatically finished at the table. An extra thick slab of premium beef—large enough to serve at least four people—is slowly roasted on a grill and presented to the table with a classic group of ingredients: arugula leaves, extra virgin olive oil, lemon zest and juice, shaved Parmigiano Reggiano cheese, sea salt and freshly cracked peppercorns. The meat is thinly sliced and draped over a salad of sorts. The results are authentically Italian, spectacularly delicious and a great way to satisfy your primal beef craving and show off at your next dinner party. SERVES 4

one 2 lb (1 kg) striploin, 4 inches
  (10 cm) thick
8 cloves of garlic
1 tablespoon (15 mL) of dried oregano
a few splashes of premium extra
  virgin olive oil, more for finishing
a sprinkle or two of sea salt and freshly
  ground pepper, more for finishing

4 handfuls or more of baby
  arugula leaves
a handful or two of fresh basil leaves
zest and juice of 1 lemon
a large chunk of authentic
  Parmigiano Reggiano

Several hours before you wish to serve dinner, purée the garlic and oregano with a few splashes of the olive oil. Slather this marinade all over the steak.

When you are ready to cook, preheat your grill to its highest setting. Season the steak with salt and pepper and begin slowly grilling it. Take your time and keep an eye on the grill heat, adjusting it to prevent burning. Flip steak as it sears. Once it has browned, flip it frequently to further prevent burning. To cook a piece of beef this large well done would be criminal! It should be cooked to medium-rare or rare to maximize its juiciness, about 20 minutes or more.

Once it's done, turn off the heat and rest the steak for 10 minutes or so, giving the meat a chance to relax and re-absorb all of its moisture. Premature slicing will release agitated hot moisture that is lost as juice.

> Order your striploin ahead of time from your specialty butcher, and ask for a large one that has the bone in. Use your best judgment to gauge doneness. Poking, prodding, pinching, probing, even peeking. A meat thermometer works well, but even a sneak peek at the interior is better than guessing.

As the beef grills, mound the arugula and basil leaves in the middle of a large festive platter.

Present the steak to your table on a wooden cutting board with a sharp knife. Slice it very thinly and arrange the slices around the arugula. Sprinkle everything with lots of olive oil, coarse sea salt and lots and lots of coarsely ground fresh peppercorns. You may theatrically zest the lemon over the salad, then squeeze on the juice. Last, but not least, use a vegetable peeler to garnish the works with shavings of Parmigiano Reggiano.

POULTRY, PORK & LAMB

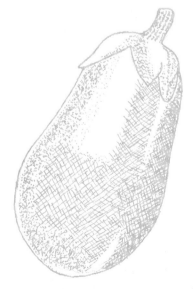

CLASSIC CHICKEN STEW

There are as many ways to stew a chicken as there are cooks and cuisines. A bowl full of this classic comfort food is the perfect antidote for anything stressful life throws your way. It's also a simple, tasty way to stretch a single chicken into a meal for many. SERVES 6 TO 8

one 4 lb (1.8 kg) roasting chicken
1 stick (½ cup/125 mL) of butter
2 onions, chopped
4 cloves of garlic, minced
½ cup (125 mL) of all-purpose flour
2 cups (500 mL) of chicken broth (see
    page 24 for homemade)
2 carrots, diced
2 stalks of celery, diced
a handful of sliced mushrooms

1 teaspoon (5 mL) of minced fresh
    thyme or rosemary
2 or 3 bay leaves
a sprinkle or two of sea salt and freshly
    ground pepper
½ cup (125 mL) of heavy cream (35%)
    or sour cream
2 or 3 green onions, thinly sliced
1 cup (250 mL) of frozen peas

For some exotic flavour, add 1 table-spoon (15 mL) or so of curry powder along with the chicken broth. For some Mediterranean flavour, omit the flour and replace the chicken broth with one 28 oz (796 mL) can of whole tomatoes. Stir in lots of fresh or dried oregano to finish.

Cut chicken into 10 pieces (2 thighs, 2 drums, 2 wings and 4 breast pieces).

Place a large heavy saucepan over medium heat and toss in the butter. Add a single layer of chicken pieces and patiently brown them until they're caramelized on all sides. Remove from the pan and rest on a plate. Repeat with any remaining chicken. By cooking the chicken in batches you avoid cooling the pan below the high heat needed for caramelization.

When the chicken is browned, add the onions to the fat and juices remaining in the pan. Sauté until golden brown and caramelized. Add the garlic and sauté a few moments longer. Stir in the flour and then whisk in the chicken broth. Bring to a simmer, whisking constantly until thickened.

Add the vegetables, fresh herbs, bay leaves and reserved chicken and any juices from the resting plate. Season with salt and pepper. Continue cooking over medium heat until the stew returns to a simmer, then turn the heat down to low, just enough to maintain the simmer.

Cover tightly and continue cooking for 30 minutes or so.

Stir in the cream, green onions and peas. Taste and add additional salt and pepper, if desired. Serve immediately or refrigerate for 2 or 3 days, then reheat when needed.

APPLE ROAST CHICKEN

A perfectly roasted chicken is the essence of home cooking, especially when the chicken and its fixings are raised responsibly on a nearby farm. In the fall my family really enjoys this aromatic dish. As the chicken roasts, the apples "melt" and form a tasty rustic pan stew that is perfect tossed with the roast chicken. This is a very easy way to cook and serve a chicken. SERVES 4 TO 6

4 local apples, quartered and cored
2 onions, peeled and cut into
   large chunks
1 whole head of garlic cloves, peeled
1 or 2 sprigs of fresh rosemary

a sprinkle or two of sea salt and
   freshly ground pepper
½ cup (125 mL) of apple cider
one 4 lb (1.8 kg) roasting chicken
2 green onions, thinly sliced

Any choice of apple will work well. For an upscale presentation, you may also slice the chicken and arrange it on a serving platter with the apple pan sauce served on the side. For an easy chicken broth, the chicken carcass can be tossed into a small stockpot with an onion, celery, carrot and bay leaf, covered with water and then simmered for 1 or 2 hours.

Preheat your oven to 350°F (180°C).

Toss the apples, onions, garlic and rosemary together in a roasting pan large enough to hold the chicken.

Season chicken well with salt and pepper and rest it on top of the apple mixture. Pour in the cider. Roast chicken until a meat thermometer inserted in the thickest part of one of the thighs reads 180°F (82°C), about 20 minutes per pound.

As soon as the chicken is cool enough to handle, and without removing it from the pan, slice and pull the meat from the carcass and toss with the apple pan stew. Remove the carcass. Sprinkle with the sliced green onions and serve directly out of the pan.

OVEN-BAKED CHICKEN
WITH SPINACH & TOMATOES

Usually when you're cooking a whole chicken, the focus is on the crispy skin, but what if the goal is deeply flavoured moist chicken meat instead? Baking in a tightly covered pot is the answer. It also happens to be one of the simplest ways to cook a chicken, and the tastiest, because this covered cooking method makes lots of true, concentrated chicken flavour. SERVES 4 TO 6

2 onions, peeled and chopped

6 cloves of garlic, peeled

2 stalks of celery, chopped

1 large carrot, peeled and chopped

a sprinkle or two of sea salt and freshly ground pepper

1 or 2 sprigs of fresh rosemary, tarragon, oregano or thyme

2 or 3 bay leaves

one 4 lb (1.8 kg) roasting chicken

1 lb (500 g) of baby spinach

2 dozen or so cherry tomatoes

Preheat your oven to 300°F (150°C).

Toss the onions, garlic, celery and carrot into a Dutch oven and lightly season them with salt and pepper. Add the rosemary and bay leaves. Stir everything together.

Season the chicken and rest it on top of the vegetables. Cover the pot tightly with a tight-fitting lid and bake the chicken for 90 minutes or so, until a thermometer inserted in one of the thighs reads 180°F (82°C).

Remove the chicken and rest on a plate, covered with foil for 15 minutes or so before slicing.

Meanwhile, place the Dutch oven over medium-high heat and bring the onion mixture to a simmer. Add the spinach and tomatoes and stir until the spinach has wilted and the tomatoes have heated through. Season to taste.

Slice the chicken, removing all the meat. Toss the meat with the spinach and tomato mixture. Serve immediately.

GRILLED CHICKEN WITH TEN TOPPINGS

Few things in your kitchen are as simple as grilling a few chicken breasts and topping them with simple flavours. It's a basic method, which always inspires improvisation as you create your own toppings with your favourite flavours. SERVES 4

4 boneless, skinless chicken breasts
a splash of any vegetable oil

a sprinkle or two of sea salt and freshly
ground pepper
the topping of your choice

Preheat your grill to its highest setting.

Lightly oil and season the chicken breasts. When the grill is hot, position the chicken breasts at a 45-degree angle to the grill's grates. After a few minutes, rotate the breasts 90 degrees for a perfect steakhouse look. After another few minutes, flip them over and repeat on the second side. Serve immediately with your favourite topping or use one of the following variations.

freestyle VARIATIONS

1. Spicy Fresh Salsa (page 248)
2. Basil Pesto (page 246)
3. Chimichurri Sauce (page 246)
4. Black olive tapenade
5. Sautéed onions finished with a dollop of mustard
6. A chopped tomato or two sautéed in olive oil with a sliced onion and minced garlic, finished with a sprinkling of oregano
7. A handful of sliced mushrooms sautéed in butter, a sprinkling of tarragon and a splash of sherry
8. A spoonful or two of tomato or pizza sauce with a sprinkle of shredded mozzarella cheese and baked or broiled for a few minutes longer
9. A chopped apple sautéed in olive oil with a sliced onion, a sprinkling of cinnamon and finished with a splash of apple juice and a spoonful of mustard
10. A dollop of peanut butter, a splash of soy sauce, a few drops of sesame oil, a spoonful of honey, the zest and juice of 1 lime and a few dashes of your favourite hot sauce stirred together

BUTTERMILK FRIED CHICKEN

Fried chicken is one of the all-time great comfort foods! For old-school flavour, try using tangy buttermilk and fry in a cast iron skillet. Nothing does a better job maintaining an even heat for crisping the chicken. SERVES 4

1 whole chicken
a sprinkle or two of sea salt
   and freshly ground pepper
2 cups (500 mL) of buttermilk
2 cups (500 mL) of all-purpose flour

2 teaspoons (10 mL) of salt
1 teaspoon (5 mL) of ground
   black pepper
2 cups (500 mL) of vegetable
   shortening

Cut chicken into 10 pieces (2 thighs, 2 drums, 2 wings and 4 breast pieces).

Put pieces into a large bowl or a resealable plastic bag and season well with salt and pepper. Pour in the buttermilk. Massage the buttermilk into the chicken pieces and then place in the refrigerator. For the best results, marinate overnight or, at the very least, for several hours.

Fit a paper lunch bag into a second paper bag, forming a double layer of paper. Pour in the flour and salt and pepper. Shake well to combine the flour and seasoning.

Drain the chicken pieces well after marinating and then add them to the bag of flour, a few at a time. Shake well to coat the pieces, remove and rest them on a rack. Repeat until all the pieces are coated well with the seasoned flour. For best results, let the coated chicken dry at room temperature for 15 or 20 minutes or so to help it get crispy during frying.

Melt the shortening in a large, cast iron skillet over medium-high heat. This type of traditional pan does the best job because it evenly heats the fat so the chicken won't burn or cook unevenly. There should be enough melted shortening to cover the pan with about a ½ inch (1 cm). Continue heating until the corner of a piece of chicken dipped into the fat causes lots of vigorous bubbling.

Add the chicken pieces in a single layer and fry them on one side until golden and crispy, about 10 minutes. If you have a lid for the pan, use it while the first side cooks but remove it once you flip the pieces so they don't get soggy.

Using tongs, turn the chicken and cook on the other side until golden and cooked through, approximately 20 minutes for both sides. Drain well on paper towels.

freestyle VARIATION

Some cooks like to season their flour with a secret blend of herbs and spices, so feel free to experiment with your own blend. Try onion powder, garlic powder, dried sage or thyme or even red chili pepper flakes, paprika or chili powder.

BRINED HOLIDAY TURKEY WITH HERB GRAVY

What's the secret to your best-tasting, juiciest holiday turkey ever? Brining—a centuries-old trick that the pros use. Soaking the turkey in salt water is simple and it really works. Brining encourages the tightly wound proteins in the meat to uncoil, bump into each other and form a web of sorts that sets in the heat of the oven, trapping flavourful moisture. Don't worry though, you don't have to be a scientist to appreciate how tasty this turkey will be. SERVES 10 OR MORE

BRINED TURKEY
one 10 to 25 lb (4.5 to 11.25 kg)
   fresh turkey
2 cups (500 mL) of table salt
   or 4 cups (1 L) of kosher salt
2 cups (500 mL) of brown sugar
2 gallons (7.25 L) of cold water
4 onions, peeled and halved
4 large carrots
4 stalks of celery
½ stick (¼ cup/60 mL)
   of butter, melted
lots of freshly ground black pepper

TOOLS NEEDED
an insulated picnic cooler large enough
   to submerge the turkey
a few "blue ice" freezer packs, placed
   in freezer bags to keep packs from
   being contaminated
a large roasting pan
an accurate meat thermometer
   to gauge exactly when the turkey
   is done

Place the bird upside down in the insulated cooler.

Whisk the salt and sugar in the cold water until they are thoroughly dissolved. Pour this brine over the turkey, turning the bird a few times to mix the salt and sugar thoroughly. If it is not fully submerged, make a bit more brine using the same ratio of salt, sugar and water. Add the freezer packs to the cooler and place in a cool place for 12 hours or overnight.

Preheat the oven to 400°F (200°C).

Remove the turkey from the brine and rinse well under cold running water. Thoroughly dry it with paper towels or clean kitchen towels. Remove any excess moisture and dry out the skin so that it will brown well.

With the onions, carrots and celery, fashion a bed in the roasting pan for the turkey to rest on. Brush the turkey thoroughly with the melted butter. Season with lots of freshly ground pepper but not salt; the brine is sufficient for salting.

continued on page 102 . . .

For an extra special treat, you can use apple cider instead of water to brine the turkey. You can also infuse the brine with a few cups of pickling spices by heating the spices in the brine a day or two in advance. (Cool it completely before using it.)

Roast turkey for 1 hour and then, without opening the oven, turn the heat down to 300°F (150°C) and continue roasting for 2 to 3 hours longer, depending on the size of the turkey. This dual-temperature method will first brown the turkey and then slowly finish it so it doesn't dry out from the initial high heat.

After 2½ hours, open the oven and begin checking the temperature every 15 minutes or so. Continue roasting until the breast and thigh meat have both reached at least 170°F (77°C). As a rough guideline you can plan on about 12 minutes cooking time for each pound of turkey.

When done, cover the turkey with foil and let rest for 20 to 30 minutes before carving to give the juices inside the meat a chance to calm down and evenly redistribute themselves throughout the turkey.

Carving & Bones

The golden rule of turkey carving is that as long as you get all the meat off the bird and onto your guest plates you've done it correctly. For an extra-special special tableside presentation try carving the turkey in the kitchen. Cut the legs off the bird and set them aside, and do the same with the wings. Carefully remove the roasted skin in one large piece. Cut each breast off the carcass then slice each one thinly and arrange on a large serving platter. Cover the breast meat with the skin and position the legs and wings so the results resemble the original bird. Garnish with a few herbs sprigs and a handful of cranberries.

HERB GRAVY

Many of the guests at my table believe the turkey is really just an elaborate premise to make gravy. This basic method relies on super-simple cornstarch to do the thickening, and there's room for enough freestyle flavour that you may end up calling the results a "sauce"! MAKES 4 CUPS OR SO

3 cups (750 mL) of water, chicken
   broth (see page 24 for homemade)
   or cider
1 cup (250 mL) of whatever wine
   you're drinking

2 tablespoons (30 mL) of cornstarch
1 tablespoon (15 mL) or so of minced
   fresh thyme, tarragon, rosemary
   or chives
salt and pepper

For the all-important gravy, pour off most of any accumulated fat, carefully reserving the juices. Add the water (or chicken broth or cider) to the pan along with the wine and any reserved juices, scraping the bottom of the pan to dissolve all of the browned bits. Pour all of the liquid into a small saucepan, scraping every last bit of flavour out of the pan. Bring it to a simmer.

    Dissolve the cornstarch in a splash of water and add to the pan, whisking until the gravy thickens. Whisk in some fresh herbs, then taste, season with salt and pepper and enjoy!

Instead of wine feel free to try sherry, Madeira, Marsala, vermouth or port. For a personalized flavour touch try stirring mustard, jam, jelly, horse-radish, chutney or your favourite condiment into the finished gravy. If you do choose something sweet it's always a good idea to add a small splash of any vinegar to balance the results.

BAKED HAM WITH TEN VARIATIONS

Because ham is so versatile, our Sunday ham tradition means a different flavour every week. Baked ham is easy to prepare, and easy to personalize with the flavour of your choice, because it goes so well with so many ingredients, including the ten variations detailed here. SERVES 6 TO 8

one 4 lb (1.8 kg) ham, bone in, labelled
 "Cook Before Eating"
2 cups (500 mL) of any liquid, such as
 fruit juice, wine or meat broth
2 heaping tablespoons (30 mL) of
 your favourite condiment: mustard,
 horseradish, marmalade, jam, jelly,
 chutney, etc.

1 tablespoon (15 mL) of any fresh herb
 or 1 teaspoon (5 mL) of any spice
2 tablespoons (30 mL) of water
1 tablespoon (15 mL) of cornstarch
a sprinkle or two of sea salt and freshly
 ground pepper

Place the ham in a large pot with a tight-fitting lid. Add your choice of liquid, condiment and herb or spice (see Variation) and, uncovered, bring to a simmer. Cover with a tight-fitting lid and continue simmering for 90 minutes or so. The ham is done when it reaches an internal temperature of 160°F (71°C). At this point you may serve the ham as is, with the broth, or you may glaze it, bake it in the oven and serve it with a sauce.

Preheat your oven to 375°F (190°C).

Remove the ham from the simmering liquid and place it in a roasting pan or large saucepan on top of the stove. Score the top with a knife. Pour 1 cup (250 mL) of the broth into another smaller saucepan. Bring it to a boil and continue cooking, reducing it over high heat until it is the consistency of syrup. Brush the glaze all over the ham and then roast it in the oven for 30 minutes, basting once or twice with more glaze.

For the sauce, dissolve the cornstarch in the 2 Tbsp (30 mL) of water. Heat the remaining ham broth to a simmer and slowly whisk in the cornstarch slurry. Stir until thickened. Taste and season as needed with salt and pepper. Once the ham is done, remove it from the oven and let it rest for 15 minutes before slicing and serving with the sauce.

freestyle
VARIATION

1. Apple juice, grainy mustard
   and rosemary
2. Apple juice, apple butter and cinnamon
3. Orange juice, marmalade
   and curry powder
4. Orange juice, horseradish and dill
5. Orange juice, brown sugar and nutmeg

6. Pineapple juice, marmalade and allspice
7. Red wine, raspberry jelly
   and ground cloves
8. White wine, grape jelly and tarragon
9. Rum, raisins and allspice
10. Chicken broth, Dijon mustard
    and rosemary

ORANGE MUSTARD GRILLED PORK TENDERLOIN

Pork tenderloin is a very tender and versatile meat that easily absorbs whatever flavour you're in the mood for, like orange mustard marinade. It's perfect for your grill! SERVES 4

2 pork tenderloins
½ cup (125 mL) of frozen orange
   juice concentrate

½ cup (125 mL) of grainy mustard
a sprinkle or two of sea salt
   and freshly ground pepper

Whisk the orange juice concentrate and mustard together. Season the pork tenderloins with salt and pepper, pour the marinade over them and marinate for a few hours, or even overnight.

Preheat your barbecue to its highest setting.

Grill the tenderloins for 10 minutes or so on each side, until a meat thermometer inserted into the thickest part reads 155°F (68°C). Let rest for 5 or 10 minutes before slicing.

freestyle VARIATION

You can add some personalized flavour to the marinade with the spice of your choice. Ground cumin, coriander, ginger, chili powder and curry powder are all excellent choices. Instead of grilling, feel free to roast this pork loin in a 400°F (200°C) oven for 20 minutes.

PAN-ROASTED PORK CHOPS
WITH ROSEMARY APPLESAUCE

Today's mainstream pork is very lean, so it can dry out quickly as it cooks. The trick to tender pork chops that stay moist and juicy is a simple two-step cooking method. Begin cooking with high heat, then finish, covered, with low heat. And a savoury twist on classic applesauce won't hurt either! SERVES 4

APPLESAUCE
¼ cup (60 mL) of olive oil
4 onions, peeled and thinly sliced
4 of your favourite apples, cored and
    cut into chunks
¼ cup (60 mL) of apple cider vinegar
1 tablespoon (15 mL) of fresh rosemary
a sprinkle or two of sea salt and freshly
    ground pepper

PAN-ROASTED PORK CHOPS
4 thick centre-loin pork chops
2 tablespoons (30 mL) of butter
1 tablespoon (15 mL) of any
    vegetable oil
a sprinkle or two of sea salt and
    freshly ground pepper

Try adding a spoonful or two of grainy mustard or horseradish to the applesauce.

For the applesauce, heat the oil in a small saucepan. Add the onions and patiently cook them, stirring occasionally, until they are caramelized and turn golden brown. Add the apple chunks, apple cider vinegar, rosemary and salt and pepper. Stir well. Simmer until the apples are very soft. Serve warm, or refrigerate and serve chilled.

For the pork chops, preheat a large sauté pan over medium-high heat. Splash in the oil and toss the butter into the centre of the oil. This will help keep the butter from burning. Pause until the butter begins to brown.

Meanwhile, pat the chops dry using paper towels, then season them with salt and pepper and carefully place them into the hot pan. Sear for 2 minutes or so on each side. Reduce heat to medium-low, cover and cook for another 10 minutes.

GRILLED LEG OF LAMB
WITH TOMATO MINT TAPENADE

The sunny flavours of the Mediterranean and the flavour of a live wood fire in my backyard make this one of my favourite ways to serve lamb. It's a great excuse to fire up your grill—any time of year. Both the marinade and the tapenade are wonderful with any type of meat or fish. SERVES 6 WITH LEFTOVERS

LAMB

1 boneless leg of lamb
1 cup (250 mL) of olive oil
2 tablespoons (30 mL) of dried
    oregano
6 or 8 cloves of garlic, minced
zest and juice of 2 lemons
several heaping spoonfuls of any
    mustard (I prefer grainy!)
a sprinkle or two of sea salt and freshly
    ground pepper

TAPENADE

a handful of sun-dried tomatoes
a handful of pitted kalamata olives
a few anchovies (optional)
zest and juice of 1 lemon
1 or 2 cloves of garlic, minced
a generous splash of extra virgin
    olive oil
a handful of mint leaves
2 tablespoons (30 mL) of capers,
    drained

If you don't have a grill, you may simply roast the lamb at 400°F (200°C) for 45 minutes or so. A tapenade is a Mediterranean condiment that traditionally includes olives, capers and anchovies but, if you don't like anchovies, leave them out!

To prepare the lamb, open the leg up into 1 large piece by cutting through the centre hole where the bone was removed. It's okay if you end up with 2 pieces. Because the meat is now thinner it will be easier to grill. Place leg in a large bowl or dish.

In a smaller dish, vigorously whisk the olive oil, oregano, garlic, lemon zest and juice, mustard and salt and pepper together until a smooth marinade forms. Add the marinade to the lamb, and rub it all over the meat. Cover the bowl or dish with plastic wrap and marinate the meat in the refrigerator for at least 1 hour. For maximum flavour marinate it for 12 hours, turning it a few times.

For the tapenade, toss the tomatoes, olives, anchovies if using, lemon zest and juice, garlic, olive oil and mint into a food processor and purée well. Stir in the capers last so they keep their shape.

To grill the lamb, build a wood fire and let it die down to a hot bed of coals, or preheat your grill to its highest setting.

For medium-rare, grill the lamb for 15 minutes or so on the first side and then another 10 minutes or so on the other side. To check the doneness, feel free to cut a small slit into the thickest part and have a peek.

Before you slice the meat, let it rest on a rack for at least 10 minutes. Heat stresses out the meat. Resting it for a few minutes allows the fibres to relax so when you slice away, you don't lose any of the juices. For best results use a cooling rack. A plate works too, but you'll lose a bit of juice where it touches the meat.

Serve with the tapenade and enjoy all the sunny flavours!

FISH & SEAFOOD

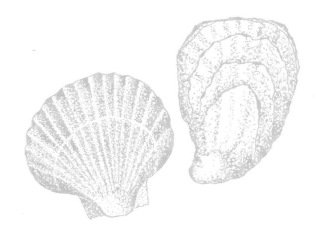

BLOODY MARY–STEAMED SALMON

One of the easiest ways to cook any type of fish is to simply simmer it in a flavourful liquid. And if that liquid just happens to taste like a classic cocktail, all the better! This dish tastes like a special occasion, but you can actually put it together in minutes. SERVES 4

4 salmon fillets, about 6 oz (175 g) each
lots of sea salt and freshly ground pepper
2 cups (500 mL) of tomato juice
½ cup (125 mL) of your finest vodka
1 tablespoon (15 mL) of horseradish
1 tablespoon (15 mL) of Worcestershire sauce
zest and juice of 1 lemon
a splash or two of olive oil
2 stalks of celery, chopped

Season the salmon fillets with lots of salt and pepper.

In a shallow saucepan with a tight-fitting lid, mix the tomato juice, vodka, horseradish, Worcestershire sauce, lemon zest and juice, olive oil and celery. Bring to a gentle simmer and then add the salmon fillets. Cover and poach the salmon in the flavourful liquid until it is just cooked through, about 10 minutes or so.

Serve each fillet in a bowl with the broth ladled overtop.

Freestyle VARIATION

When you cook, all flavour molecules dissolve in either water, fat or alcohol. In this dish the vodka highlights an additional layer of flavours in the tomato. You may substitute an aromatic gin for a pleasant pungent flavour. Try filling the bowls with a handful of baby spinach before adding the salmon and broth.

CORNMEAL-CRUSTED SALMON WITH BASIL MUSSEL BROTH

Salmon—farmed or wild—is one of the healthiest ingredients in any kitchen, and one of the most versatile. It's easy to add a crisp cornmeal crust and a rich aromatic mussel broth! SERVES 4

2 to 3 lb (1 to 1.5 kg) of fresh mussels, rinsed well in cold running water
a big splash of any white wine
a big splash of heavy cream (35%)
2 tablespoons (30 mL) of Basil Pesto (page 246)

1 cup (250 mL) or so of fine cornmeal
a sprinkle or two of sea salt and freshly ground pepper
4 skinless salmon fillets, about 6 oz (175 g) each
a big splash of vegetable oil

To make the broth, wash the mussels very well and discard any that are open and won't close with a bit of gentle finger pressure.

Toss the mussels, wine and cream into a large stockpot and begin cooking over medium-high heat. Cover the pot with a tight-fitting lid to capture the steam. Cook until the mussel shells pop open, about 5 minutes or so. Cool the mussels until you can handle them, then shuck away, tossing the shells and any lingering fibres.

{ Most mussels are sold without their beards, the tough fibres they use to anchor themselves to rocks under water. If your mussels' beards are still attached, just tug them off.

Strain the broth into a saucepan. When you're ready to serve the salmon, bring the broth to a simmer, season it and then stir in the basil pesto and reserved mussel meat.

To make the crust on the salmon, pour the finely ground cornmeal into a large resealable bag with a sprinkle of salt and a generous sprinkle of pepper. (When you're crusting something, coarsely ground cornmeal doesn't adhere as well as finely ground cornmeal.) Toss each salmon fillet one at a time with the cornmeal.

Preheat a large sauté pan over medium-high heat for a few minutes.

Add a big splash of cooking oil, enough to cover the bottom of the pan in a thin film. When you're pan-frying the fish, it's better to have a bit too much oil rather than too little. This will help the crust cook more evenly. Carefully add the crusted fillets and pan-fry until crisp and golden on the first side, about 5 minutes. Turn the fillets and crisp the other side.

Serve with a ladleful of the reheated mussel broth.

You can flavour the mussel broth with any wine. The cream is optional—it adds richness, but the broth is still very flavourful without it. You may replace the basil pesto with a spoonful of any herb you fancy. For a flavour twist, try adding chili powder, curry powder or fennel or poppy seeds to the cornmeal. Try filling your bowl with a handful or two of baby spinach leaves before adding the salmon and broth.

GRILLED SALMON BURGERS
WITH PICKLED RED ONIONS

Who says burgers have to be made from meat? You'll be amazed at how easy these are to put together, and your guests will be impressed with how tasty they are. They're packed full of Asian-inspired flavour, a great way to jazz up your next barbecue excursion with something different and healthy. SERVES 4

1 lb (500 g) of salmon fillets, skin
   removed, then cubed
2 cups (500 mL) of cilantro leaves
¼ cup (60 mL) of minced red onion
¼ cup (60 mL) of grated frozen ginger

1 tablespoon (15 mL) of soy sauce
1 teaspoon (5 mL) of sriracha or
   your favourite hot sauce
a splash of any vegetable oil

Toss the salmon, cilantro, red onion, ginger, soy sauce, hot sauce and vegetable oil into a food processor and pulse for a few seconds, a few times, just until the ingredients come together. The mixture will still be a bit chunky and even seem a bit wet. Do not purée!

Preheat your barbecue to its highest setting.

Form the mixture into 4 evenly shaped and evenly thick patties. The burgers may seem like they'll fall apart on the grill, but don't worry—they'll be nice and firm once they cook through.

Place the burgers on the grill and cook until golden brown on the first side. Flip them over and brown the other side. Serve alone or on a bun with your favourite burger condiments.

Serve with Pickled Red Onions (page 248).

Freestyle VARIATION

You can add lots of Mediterranean flair to these burgers by substituting tomato paste, salt and pepper and fresh or dried oregano for the ginger, soy sauce, hot sauce and cilantro.

MAPLE MUSTARD GRILLED SALMON

Salmon is a regular guest at our table, often grilled with this simple sauce. Its sweet and pungent flavour easily stands up to the richness of the fish. Whenever possible we choose wild Pacific salmon; it's the most sustainable choice available. We're also big fans of farm-raised Atlantic salmon. It's much better for us, and the environment, than beef or meat every day. SERVES 4

4 salmon fillets, about 6 oz
   (175 g) each
lots of sea salt and freshly
   ground pepper

½ cup (125 mL) of maple syrup
½ cup (125 mL) of grainy mustard

Season the salmon fillets with lots of salt and pepper.

Whisk the maple syrup and mustard together. Place the salmon in a small pan or resealable plastic bag. Pour the marinade over the salmon and marinate for 1 or 2 hours, or even overnight.

Build a hardwood fire and let it die down to a thick bed of glowing coals, or preheat your barbecue to its highest setting.

Grill the salmon fillets for about 5 minutes on the first side, a little less on the second side. Serve at once.

You can easily bake this fish as well. Just pop it into a preheated 400°F (200°C) oven for 12 minutes or so. You can personalize the marinade a bit as well by adding 1 teaspoon (5 mL) of curry powder or chili powder. You can also substitute honey for the maple syrup.

PROSCIUTTO-WRAPPED SALMON

Wrapping prosciutto around salmon fillets is an easy way to dress up fish while adding some intense flavour and bringing flair to your table. The prosciutto is very easy to work with. It actually "shrink wraps" as it cooks, tightly sealing itself to the fish. It's a spectacular presentation and very tasty.

SERVES 4

4 salmon fillets, about 6 oz
   (175 g) each
a sprinkle or two of sea salt and
   freshly ground pepper

¼ cup (60 mL) of grainy mustard
4 slices of prosciutto

Preheat your oven to 375°F (190°C).

Meanwhile, season the salmon fillets with a sprinkle of salt and pepper. Evenly spread the mustard on the top surface of each fillet. Tightly roll each fillet in a slice of prosciutto so that the end is weighed down beneath the salmon. The fillet should be sitting on the seam, and the ends of the salmon will protrude beyond the prosciutto.

Place wrapped fillets on a baking pan, seam side down. Bake until done, about 15 minutes.

This dish is also very good with pesto (page 246), tapenade or hummus spread (page 19) on the fish instead of the mustard. This technique also works very well with chicken breasts.

PAN-FRIED WHITEFISH

This is one of the easiest ways to cook any type of fish. It's also one of the tastiest, and fastest. Perhaps more than any other technique, this is how I choose to get fish on the table in a hurry. Whitefish is a generic term that refers to many different types of fish, all of them easy to find and cook. SERVES 4 TO 6

1 cup (250 mL) of whole wheat
    or any flour
a sprinkle or two of sea salt
    and freshly ground pepper
1 tablespoon (15 mL) of paprika
1 tablespoon (15 mL) of any dried
    herb or spice

juice of 1 lemon
4 to 6 whitefish fillets, about
    2 lb (1 kg) total
a large splash of any vegetable oil
2 tablespoons (30 mL) of butter

This method is excellent for any whitefish: halibut, hake, haddock, sole, cod, flounder or tilapia. You can add lots of personalized flavour to the seasoned flour. Try replacing half or more of the flour with fine cornmeal. Dill, thyme, tarragon and oregano all work well as fresh herbs while chili powder, curry powder, ground cumin and red pepper flakes all make excellent spices. My all-time favourite addition, though, is a paprika-based spice blend commonly found along the southern Atlantic coastline: Old Bay Seasoning.

Preheat your largest, heaviest sauté pan or skillet over medium-high heat. A heavier pan will distribute the heat more evenly than a thin one.

Whisk together the flour, salt and pepper, paprika and herb.

Pour the seasoned flour into a shallow dish large enough to hold 1 or 2 fish fillets. Depending on the size of the fillets, and your guests' inclination to share, cut the fish into individual portions or leave whole. Dredge fillet pieces in the seasoned flour until they are evenly coated. Rest on a pan or plate but don't stack them on top of one another.

Pour a large splash of vegetable oil into the pan, enough to cover the pan's bottom in a thin film. Add the butter to the centre of the oil. The oil will protect the delicate butter from burning, and the butter will add lots of brown flavour. When the butter begins to brown and sizzle, swirl it around the pan and quickly add the fish fillets. Turn up the heat, adjusting it as needed to keep the pan sizzling hot.

Cook the fish in batches so they all brown evenly. Cook the first side of the fillets for a few minutes until they're golden brown and beautiful. Carefully flip them and continue with the other side. You may find it useful to add a bit more butter after you flip the fish over.

Continue until the fish cooks through. Add the lemon juice and swirl the pan. It will sizzle, form a quick sauce with the butter and coat each fillet. Serve immediately.

WHITEFISH PROVENÇALE

When a local fisherman shows up at my door with a fresh halibut, this is the gold standard recipe I reach for. It's my favourite way to add lots of simple, bright Mediterranean flavour to the firm, meaty whitefish. This dish is spectacular enough for a special occasion but easy enough for a quick weeknight dinner. SERVES 4

a splash of extra virgin olive oil

4 fresh halibut or other whitefish fillets, 5 to 6 oz (150 to 175 g) each

a sprinkle or two of sea salt and freshly ground pepper

4 large ripe local tomatoes or one 28 oz (796 mL) can of whole tomatoes

1 large onion, minced

4 large cloves of garlic, minced

½ cup (125 mL) of capers, drained

½ cup (125 mL) of pitted kalamata olives

½ cup (125 mL) of pitted green olives

2 tablespoons (30 mL) of balsamic vinegar

1 tablespoon (15 mL) of minced fresh oregano or 1 teaspoon (5 mL) of dried

Preheat a large, heavy skillet over medium-high heat. Add a splash of olive oil, enough to cover the bottom of the pan with a thin film.

Pat the halibut fillets dry with a piece of paper towel and then lightly season them with salt and pepper.

Carefully place the fillets in the hot oil and sear on both sides, patiently browning them until they are golden brown and beautiful. They don't have to cook all the way through at this point.

Remove the fillets from the pan and add the tomatoes, onion, garlic, capers, olives, vinegar and oregano. Bring the mixture to a vigorous simmer, then return the halibut to the pan and lower the heat a bit. Nestle the fillets into the tomato mixture and continue cooking until they are cooked through, just a few minutes longer. Serve the halibut with several generous spoonfuls of the tomato mixture.

This method is excellent for any whitefish: halibut, hake, haddock, sole, cod, flounder or tilapia. Try adding a few large spoonfuls of pesto (page 246) instead of the oregano. You can easily substitute the zest and juice of a lemon for the balsamic vinegar. Sometimes I like to add a head of chopped fennel to this dish. If you use fresh oregano, save a few sprigs for a garnish.

POTATO FISH CAKES

Historically, fish cakes have been one of the most common ways to eat fish in the Maritime provinces of Canada. Usually they were made with preserved salt cod, but today they're much tastier with fresh salmon. These crispy cakes are as easy to make as they are to enjoy. SERVES 4

a splash or two of vegetable oil
2 fillets of salmon, or any other fish, about 12 oz (375 g) in total
a sprinkle or two of sea salt and freshly ground pepper
4 large baking potatoes, peeled
2 eggs, whisked together
1 tablespoon (15 mL) of Dijon mustard

2 green onions, thinly sliced
a sprinkle or two of sea salt and freshly ground pepper
2 tablespoons (30 mL) of all-purpose flour
1 to 2 tablespoons (15 to 30 mL) of butter

Freestyle VARIATION

Try adding some of your favourite fresh herbs to the mix. Tarragon, dill, parsley, oregano and thyme all work well. For a flavour twist, you may substitute horseradish for the mustard. Fish cakes are traditionally served with mustard pickles but tartar sauce, cocktail sauce and even salsa are all good as well. (See page 248 for a salsa recipe, and page 249 for Cocktail Sauce.)

Preheat a sauté pan or skillet over medium-high heat.

Add a splash of oil to the pan, enough to cover the bottom with a thin film. Season the salmon fillets with salt and pepper and carefully place in the pan. Sear the fillets on both sides until they're golden brown, crispy and cooked through.

Boil or steam the potatoes. Toss hot potatoes into a mixing bowl. Using a potato masher, mash them until smooth. Add the salmon, eggs, mustard and green onions. Season with more salt and pepper. Beat with a wooden spoon until everything is very well combined and then form the mixture into evenly shaped cakes. Dredge them in the flour.

Clean out the skillet and preheat over medium-high heat. Add another splash of oil and this time 1 to 2 tablespoons (5 to 10 mL) or so of butter. When the butter melts and sizzles, add the fish cakes. Pan-fry them until they're golden brown and crispy on both sides.

SAUTÉED SHRIMP COCKTAIL

Shrimp is the most popular seafood in North America, and topped with cocktail sauce is one of the most popular ways to serve it. This super-simple method cooks the shrimp and makes the sauce at the same time. For best results and a great sustainable choice, purchase shrimp from North America where their harvest is subject to strict regulations. Imported shrimp are often raised or trawled in a very irresponsible manner. SERVES 4

½ cup (125 mL) of olive oil
1 tablespoon (15 mL) of minced garlic
2 lb (1 kg) of large or extra large
    shrimp, peeled and deveined
zest and juice of 1 lemon
½ cup (125 mL) of chili sauce

2 ripe tomatoes, diced
¼ cup (60 mL) of horseradish
1 tablespoon (15 mL) of soy sauce
1 bunch of fresh parsley, minced
2 green onions, thinly sliced

If you can't find truly ripe tomatoes, feel free to use a few canned ones. This dish is excellent tossed with your favourite pasta or served over rice. It's also good with a handful of freshly chopped dill stirred in.

Pour the olive oil into a large skillet or sauté pan set over low heat. Add the garlic and cook, stirring occasionally, until it turns golden brown. Be patient; this is the key to the flavour of the dish.

When the whole house smells wonderful, turn the heat up to medium and immediately add the shrimp. Cook, stirring occasionally, until they begin to turn pink. Add the lemon zest and juice, chili sauce, tomatoes, horseradish and soy sauce. Turn the heat to high and bring the mixture to a simmer.

Turn off the heat and stir in the parsley and green onion.

STEAMED MUSSELS TEN WAYS

Mussels travel with their own built-in sauce base. They're easy to steam and, when you do, they release a flavourful broth that many connoisseurs swear is the best part. That broth can be flavoured any way you want, so mussels are also a great ingredient to freestyle with. SERVES 4

5 to 6 lb (2.2 to 2.7 kg) of mussels, rinsed well with cold running water
1 cup (250 mL) of any flavourful liquid

1 cup (250 mL) of any other flavourful ingredients
a splash or two of olive oil or a spoonful or so of butter

Wash the mussels very well and discard any that are open and won't close with a bit of gentle finger pressure.

Pour the liquid and other aromatic ingredients of your choice into a large pot with a tight-fitting lid. Stir to combine and bring to a simmer over medium-high heat. Add the mussels and cover with the lid. Shake the pot occasionally and cook until all the mussels have opened, 10 minutes or so. Discard any that haven't opened.

Spoon out the mussels into a serving bowl. Strain the remaining liquid to remove any bits of broken shell or lingering sand. Serve over the mussels.

1. **THAI** Coconut milk and a spoonful of Thai curry paste
2. **SOUTHWESTERN** Spicy Fresh Salsa (page 248), cilantro and a splash of tequila
3. **MEDITERRANEAN** Tomato purée, minced garlic and capers
4. **ITALIAN** Canned tomatoes, minced garlic and Basil Pesto (page 246)
5. **GREEK** Tomato juice, chopped olives, minced garlic, artichoke hearts, the zest and juice of 2 lemons, a spoonful of oregano and olive oil

6. **FRENCH** White wine, Dijon mustard and butter
7. **ENGLISH** A can of Guinness beer and sliced onions
8. **APPLE** Apple cider with a splash of apple cider vinegar
9. **JAPANESE** A few spoonfuls of soy sauce, a splash of rice wine vinegar, a few drops of sesame oil and sliced green onions
10. **CALIFORNIA** Orange juice, orange marmalade, lemon juice and diced red bell pepper

VEGETARIAN

BROWN RICE & LENTILS

This is one of Gabe's favourite dishes. It's often the centrepiece of dinner on our table. As simple to make as any rice, its hearty, earthy flavour is quite addictive and it's packed with nutritional goodness! SERVES 6 TO 8

a splash of olive oil
1 large onion, minced
4 cloves of garlic, minced
1 cup (250 mL) of brown rice
1 cup (250 mL) of dried lentils

4 cups (1 L) of chicken broth (see
   page 24 for homemade) or water
a bay leaf or two
a sprinkle or two of sea salt and
   freshly ground pepper

You may add any fresh or dried herbs you like to this dish. Rosemary, thyme and tarragon all work well. At the last second, you may also add ½ cup (125 mL) or so of raisins or some sliced green onions.

Splash the olive oil into a small pot with a tight-fitting lid over medium-high heat. Add the onion and garlic and sauté for a few minutes until they just start to turn golden brown.

Add the rice, lentils, chicken broth (or water), bay leaves and salt and pepper. Bring everything to a simmer. Cover and reduce the heat to low, just enough to maintain the simmer. Continue cooking until the rice and lentils are tender and the liquid is absorbed, about 45 minutes.

Turn off the heat and let stand for a few minutes before serving.

BULGUR & MUSHROOM BURGERS

One of the Holy Grails of vegetarian cooking is a meat-free burger that's tasty, nutritious, full of protein, easy to make and easy to handle. Without the strong protein structure of meat, or the scientific hijinks of processed burgers, it can be tricky to get vegetarian burgers to hold together though, so this burger uses the strength of bulgur wheat. It will easily become one of your favourites.

MAKES 6 LARGE OR 8 SMALL BURGERS

2 tablespoons (30 mL) of any
   vegetable oil
½ lb (250 g) of fresh shiitake mushrooms, stems removed and sliced
2 onions, chopped
4 cloves of garlic, minced
2 cups (500 mL) of water
1 cup (250 mL) of bulgur wheat
2 tablespoons (30 mL) of soy sauce

2 eggs
2 tablespoons (30 mL) of miso paste
1 cup (250 mL) of breadcrumbs
one 19 oz (540 mL) can of black
   beans, drained and rinsed
1 tablespoon (15 mL) of minced
   fresh thyme
a sprinkle or two of sea salt and
   freshly ground pepper

Splash the oil into a saucepan over medium-high heat. Add the mushrooms, onions and garlic. Sauté until the mushrooms lose their moisture and the onions caramelize, about 20 minutes. This step is one of the keys to the mixture; it is important to cook out as much moisture as possible so the burger will hold together.

Add the water, bulgur and soy sauce. Cover with a tight-fitting lid and cook over low heat until the bulgur is tender and has absorbed all the liquid, about 20 minutes.

Pour the mixture onto a plate or tray and let it cool to room temperature.

When cool, transfer the bulgur-mushroom mixture into the bowl of your food processor. Add the eggs, miso paste, breadcrumbs, black beans, thyme and salt and pepper. Purée until smooth.

Form the mixture into evenly shaped patties about 1 inch (2.5 cm) thick. Refrigerate until firm, about 1 hour.

Preheat your barbecue on its highest setting.

Lightly brush the burgers with oil and grill until they are cooked through and caramelized a bit. Alternatively, you may pan-sear them in a lightly oiled preheated pan or simply bake them at 400°F (200°C). Enjoy with your favourite burger toppings.

Try substituting a spoonful or two of chili powder for the fresh thyme.

INDIAN RICE & DAL

This is one of my favourite dishes. I love the bright curried lentil sauce and the soft fragrance of the basmati rice. Together they're addictively aromatic and one of the all-time great flavour combinations. Best of all, this dish is loaded with healthy goodness! SERVES 4

DAL

3 cups (750 mL) of water
1 cup (250 mL) of red lentils
   or yellow split peas
1 onion, diced
2 cloves of garlic, minced
1 tablespoon (15 mL) of curry powder
a sprinkle or two of sea salt
1 jalapeño pepper, finely minced
a handful of chopped cilantro

RICE

2 tablespoons (30 mL) of butter
1 onion, minced
2 or 3 cloves of garlic, minced
1 cup (250 mL) of basmati rice
2 cups (500 mL) of water
a sprinkle or two of sea salt
   and freshly ground pepper

You may serve the dal over any type of rice; basmati is traditional in India. For even more authentic Indian flavour, try adding cumin seeds to the dal. Once the dal is cooked, some cooks like to stir a few chopped tomatoes.

Make the dal first because the lentils take longer to cook than the rice. Place the water, lentils or split peas, onion, garlic, curry powder and salt in a saucepan with a tight-fitting lid. Bring everything to a simmer over medium-high heat and then reduce the heat to low—just enough to maintain the simmer. Cover and continue cooking for 30 minutes or so.

While the dal cooks, make the basmati rice. Melt the butter in another small saucepan with a tight-fitting lid. Add the onion and garlic and sauté for a few minutes until they just begin to turn golden brown. Add the rice and continue cooking for a few minutes longer, stirring constantly. This is known as the pilaf method, and it helps ensure that each finished rice grain will be tender and distinct.

Add the water and bring it to a simmer. Season the works, cover and cook over low heat until the water is absorbed and the rice is tender, about 15 minutes. Let stand for 5 minutes or so before serving.

After the dal has simmered for 30 minutes or so, remove the lid and stir. Continue simmering, partially covered, until the lentils break down into a thick purée, another 10 minutes or so. Taste and add a bit more salt if you like. Stir in the jalapeño pepper and cilantro and serve immediately over the basmati rice.

MOROCCAN COUSCOUS & CHICKPEAS

Couscous is a grain-like form of pasta made from semolina flour, the same flour used to make pasta. It's very common throughout the Mediterranean and North Africa. In Morocco it's often served with dried fruits and nuts and lots of mysterious aromatic spiciness. SERVES 4 TO 6

2 tablespoons (30 mL) of olive oil
1 onion, minced
a few cloves of garlic, minced
½ teaspoon (2 mL) of ground
    cinnamon
½ teaspoon (2 mL) of ground cumin
½ teaspoon (2 mL) of ground coriander
½ teaspoon (2 mL) of powdered ginger
one 19 oz (540 mL) can of chickpeas,
    drained and rinsed well
1 cup (250 mL) of couscous

½ cup (125 mL) of raisins
½ cup (125 mL) of dried apricots,
    sliced
2 cups (500 mL) of orange juice
zest and juice of 1 lemon
a sprinkle or two of sea salt
    and freshly ground pepper
½ cup (125 mL) of sliced
    or slivered almonds
a handful of chopped cilantro

Splash the olive oil into a small saucepan over a medium-high heat. Add the onion, garlic and spices. Sauté for a few minutes until everything is heated through and your kitchen smells fragrant.

Add the chickpeas, couscous, raisins, apricots, orange juice, lemon zest and juice, and salt and pepper. Bring everything to a simmer and then reduce the heat to low, just enough to maintain the simmer. Cover with a tight-fitting lid and continue cooking until the couscous is tender and the liquid has been absorbed, about 15 minutes.

Turn off the heat and let the couscous rest for another 5 minutes or so before serving. Using a fork to help fluff up the couscous, transfer it into a serving bowl and sprinkle with the almonds and cilantro.

In Morocco couscous is normally seasoned with a pinch of *ras el hanout*, a unique spice blend whose name means literally "top of the shop"—the spice merchant's best. If you like, you can make your own ras el hanout by combining equal parts of ground cardamom, cinnamon, cloves, coriander, cumin, ginger, allspice, nutmeg, mace, turmeric and black pepper. Use 2 teaspoons (10 mL) in total for this recipe.

SOUTHWESTERN SCRAMBLED TOFU

Tofu is a highly nutritious bean curd made from soy milk. It's an excellent source of protein and very easy to cook with. There are many varieties and many ways to cook it. Pan-frying softer tofu until it resembles scrambled eggs is one of the simplest and tastiest. SERVES 4

a splash of any vegetable oil
1 teaspoon (5 mL) of whole cumin
   seeds
1 red bell pepper, thinly sliced
1 or 2 cloves of garlic, minced
1 tomato, chopped
one 12 oz (350 g) package of soft tofu,
   cut into small pieces

1 teaspoon (5 mL) of turmeric
a handful of chopped cilantro
2 green onions, thinly sliced
a few dashes of your favourite
   hot sauce
1 tablespoon (15 mL) of sour cream
a sprinkle or two of sea salt

You may flavour scrambled tofu with many other international flavours: Asian, Creole, Thai, French or hodgepodge. You are only limited by your imagination and by what's in your fridge.

Add a splash or two of vegetable oil to a large sauté pan over medium heat. Add the cumin seeds and cook them until they're fragrant and lightly browned, about 1 or 2 minutes. Immediately add the bell pepper and garlic and continue cooking until they soften, another 3 minutes or so.

Add the tomato, the tofu and the turmeric and continue cooking, stirring constantly, until the tofu breaks up and resembles scrambled eggs, another 1 or 2 minutes.

Stir in the cilantro, green onion, hot sauce, sour cream and salt. Continue cooking just long enough to heat through.

SOUTHWESTERN BLACK BEAN & CORN CHILI

This chili is packed with so much bright Southwestern flavour that you'll never notice it doesn't include meat, but you will notice how quickly everyone empties their bowl! SERVES 8

2 tablespoons (30 mL) of any
  vegetable oil
2 large onions, chopped
1 large carrot, chopped
1 red bell pepper, chopped
1 green bell pepper, chopped
4 cloves of garlic, minced
1 chipotle pepper, packed
  in adobo sauce
1 tablespoon (15 mL) of chili powder

1 tablespoon (15 mL) of ground cumin
1 tablespoon (15 mL) of dried oregano
one 28 oz (796 mL) can of whole
  tomatoes
two 16 oz (475 mL) cans of black
  beans, drained and rinsed
2 cups (500 mL) of frozen corn
a sprinkle or two of sea salt
4 green onions, thinly sliced
a bunch of chopped cilantro

freestyle VARIATION

Chipotle chili peppers in adobo sauce are smoked jalapeño peppers packed in a highly flavourful tomato-vinegar sauce. If you don't have any chipotles, you may easily substitute 1 or 2 jalapeños. Try topping each bowl with some grated cheddar cheese.

Splash the oil into a large saucepan over medium-high heat. Add the onions, carrot, bell peppers and garlic. Sauté until the onions are golden and the vegetables have softened, about 10 minutes.

Add the chipotle pepper, chili powder, cumin and oregano. Continue cooking, stirring constantly for a few minutes longer.

Add the tomatoes, black beans, corn and salt and bring everything to a boil. Reduce the heat so it's just high enough to maintain a simmer. Continue cooking without a lid, stirring frequently, until the flavours are blended and the chili thickens, about 30 minutes.

Taste and add some more salt if you like. Just before serving, stir in the green onions and cilantro.

SOUTHWESTERN RED BEANS & BROWN RICE

This vegetarian version of a classic southern dish omits the traditional ham hock and replaces it with lots of bright Southwestern flavour. SERVES 4 TO 6

BEANS

1 lb (500 g) of dried red beans, soaked
   overnight in lots of water
a splash of any vegetable oil
2 onions, finely chopped
2 stalks of celery, finely chopped
1 red bell pepper, finely chopped
1 jalapeño pepper, finely minced
4 cloves of garlic, finely minced
1 tablespoon (15 mL) of chili powder
1 teaspoon (5 mL) of ground cumin
1 teaspoon (5 mL) of dried oregano
4 cups (1 L) of water

a sprinkle or two of sea salt and freshly
   ground pepper
4 fresh or canned tomatoes, chopped
4 green onions, sliced
a handful or two of chopped cilantro

RICE

2 tablespoons (30 mL) of butter
1 onion, minced
2 or 3 cloves of garlic, minced
1 cup (250 mL) of brown rice
2 cups (500 mL) of water
a sprinkle or two of sea salt and freshly
   ground pepper

Strain the beans out of their soaking water and give them a good rinse. No nutrients are lost in this process; instead, the beans rehydrate, which will speed up their cooking time.

Make the beans first because they take longer than the rice. Splash the oil into a saucepan with a tight-fitting lid and set over medium-high heat. Add the onions, celery, bell peppers, garlic, chili powder, cumin and oregano and sauté for a few minutes until everything is heated through and your kitchen smells wonderful. Add the red beans, water and salt and pepper and bring everything to a simmer. Reduce the heat and continue simmering, covered, until the beans are tender, about 30 to 45 minutes.

Meanwhile, make the rice. Melt the butter in another small saucepan with a tight-fitting lid. Add the onion and garlic and sauté for a few minutes until they just begin to turn golden brown. Add the rice and continue cooking for a few minutes longer, stirring constantly. This is known as the pilaf method, and it helps ensure that each finished rice grain will be tender and distinct.

Add the water and bring it to a simmer. Season the works, cover and cook over low heat until the water is absorbed and the rice is tender, about 45 minutes. Let stand for 5 minutes or so before serving.

Finish the beans by stirring in the tomatoes, green onions and cilantro. Serve over the rice.

Feel free to use your favourite chili peppers to season this dish. You can use dried red kidney, red pinto, other red beans and even black beans.

SWEET POTATO CHICKPEA CURRY

This is one of our all-time favourite dishes, a brightly flavoured bowl of half stew, half soup and all flavour. Its spicy aromas are so tasty and addictive that you'll never notice it doesn't include meat. This dish is at its best when it's served over rice. SERVES 6 TO 8

a splash of vegetable oil
1 large onion, diced
3 or 4 cloves of garlic, chopped
a small knob of frozen ginger
1 teaspoon (5 mL) of Thai curry paste
2 sweet potatoes, peeled and cubed
one 19 oz (540 mL) can of chickpeas
one 14 oz (398 mL) can
    of coconut milk

1 cup (250 mL) of orange juice
½ cup (125 mL) of peanut butter
    or any other nut butter
a sprinkle or two of sea salt
1 cup (250 mL) or so of frozen
    green peas
several handfuls of baby spinach
a bunch of chopped cilantro

Add a splash or two of vegetable oil to a stockpot over medium-high heat. Toss in the onion and garlic and sauté them until they're lightly browned, about 5 minutes or so.

Grate the frozen ginger into the pan with a Microplane grater or standard box grater and add the Thai curry paste. Continue cooking until the spices are heated through and fragrant, another few minutes.

Add the sweet potatoes, chickpeas, coconut milk, orange juice, peanut butter and salt. Bring to a simmer, lower the heat and continue simmering until the sweet potatoes are tender, about 30 minutes. Stir in the peas, spinach and cilantro.

Serve over rice.

There are three basic types of Thai curry paste, each with its own distinctive flavour. You may choose one based on your tolerance for spicy heat: yellow is the mildest, red is a bit spicier and green is the spiciest. This dish cooks very well in your slow cooker. You may use any type of hard winter squash instead of sweet potatoes; butternut and acorn work well.

TOASTED QUINOA PILAF

Quinoa (pronounced keen-wah*) is one of the healthiest foods on the planet—it's packed with vitamins, minerals and protein. It's actually a seed, but it's cooked like a grain. The rich nutty taste is perfect in a pilaf, but it's just as good stirred into any salad. Because of its flavour, ease of cooking and high nutritional value, quinoa is one of the most common foods on my table.* SERVES 4

2 tablespoons (30 mL) of olive oil
1 small onion, minced
2 cloves of garlic, minced
1 cup (250 mL) of quinoa, rinsed
    and drained

2 cups (500 mL) of chicken broth (see
    page 24 for homemade) or water
a sprinkle or two of sea salt and freshly
    ground pepper

Because of its aromatic nutty flavour, quinoa is especially good served with other nuts. We often sprinkle toasted almonds on top of this dish.

Pour the olive oil into a small saucepan with a tight-fitting lid over medium-high heat. Add the onion and garlic and sauté for a few minutes until they just begin to turn golden brown.

Add the quinoa and continue cooking for a few minutes longer, stirring constantly, until the quinoa is golden brown and toasted, about 5 minutes. This will add lots of aromatic flavour to the dish.

Pour in the chicken broth or water, season with salt and pepper and bring to a simmer. Cover and cook until the liquid has been absorbed and the quinoa has unfurled and is tender, about 15 minutes.

Let stand for about 5 minutes or so before serving.

Quinoa seeds grow with a naturally bitter coating that is easily rinsed off. In fact, most of it has been washed off before it gets to you anyway, but it's always a good idea to thoroughly rinse it once again. Pour the quinoa into a fine mesh strainer and run lots of cold water over it.

TWELVE GRAINS

Whole grains are one of the tastiest, healthiest and most versatile ingredients in your kitchen. They're also one of the easiest to cook. They simply need to simmer in water until they're tender and are ready to enjoy by themselves or as an ingredient in many other dishes.

To cook 1 cup (250 mL) of each grain, simply combine it with the amount of water indicated below and a sprinkle or two of salt. Bring the mixture to a boil and then reduce the heat just enough to maintain a simmer. Cover with a tight-fitting lid and continue cooking for the time as indicated.

Without taking off the lid, remove the pan from the heat and let stand for 10 minutes before serving.

Barley	4 cups (1 L)	45 minutes
Bulgur	2 cups (500 mL)	15 minutes
Millet	2½ cups (625 mL)	20 minutes
Oats, quick-cooking rolled	2 cups (500 mL)	5 minutes
Oats, old-fashioned rolled	4 cups (1 L)	5 minutes
Quinoa	2 cups (500 mL)	15 minutes
Rice, white	2 cups (500 mL)	25 minutes
Rice, brown long-grain	2½ cups (625 mL)	40 minutes
Rice, brown short-grain	2 cups (500 mL)	45 minutes
Rice, wild	3 cups (750 mL)	45 minutes
Rye berries	3 cups (750 mL)	50 minutes
Wheat berries	3 cups (750 mL)	90 minutes

freestyle VARIATION

As each grain cooks it may be seasoned with onions, garlic or your favourite herb. Each may be served as is, stirred into a soup or stew while still hot, or cooled and tossed into any salad.

PASTA

MACARONI & CHEESE — 158

FETTUCCINE ALFREDO — 161

SPAGHETTI WITH HIDDEN-VEGETABLE TOMATO SAUCE — 162

SPAGHETTI & MEATBALLS WITH SIMPLE TOMATO SAUCE — 164

LASAGNA WITH SPEEDY MEAT SAUCE — 167

FARFALLE WITH ROASTED TOMATO GARLIC SAUCE — 168

PENNE WITH RED PEPPER SAUCE & SPINACH — 171

PENNE WITH TOMATO BACON SAUCE — 172

PENNE WITH SMOKED SALMON & CREAM CHEESE SAUCE — 175

PASTA WITH BRAISED CHICKEN, SAUSAGES, PEPPERS & TOMATOES — 176

MACARONI & CHEESE

Few things are as good as a steaming bowl of homemade macaroni and cheese, especially when it doesn't come out of a box. There's something very satisfying about making this classic dish yourself. And it tastes a whole lot better than anything made in a factory! SERVES 4 TO 6

one 1 lb (454 g) box of penne
½ stick (¼ cup / 60 mL) of butter
2 cloves of garlic, chopped
⅔ cup (160 mL) of all-purpose flour
a big splash of white wine
4 cups (1 L) of milk
one 12 oz (354 mL) can of unsweetened evaporated milk
1 lb (454 g) of medium-aged
   cheddar cheese, shredded

2 tablespoons (30 mL)
   of Dijon mustard
1 tablespoon (15 mL) of paprika
a pinch of cayenne pepper
a sprinkle or two of sea salt
½ loaf of Italian bread, torn into
   large pieces
a generous splash of olive oil

Try substituting the cheddar with other semisoft cheeses like Swiss, Jack or Emmenthal. Just about any minced fresh herb will add a wonderful aroma to the cheese sauce. I like dill, tarragon or thyme. For an extra special decadent version, stir in the meat from several cooked lobsters.

Cooking Pasta
As pasta cooks it will absorb the salt water and, in turn, be properly seasoned. A pinch or two of salt is not enough! Taste the water; it should remind you of a day at the beach. Cook the pasta until it's al dente—tender but still quite firm in the centre; it will finish cooking in the sauce. Drain it well, but don't rinse, or you'll drain away the surface starch that helps the sauce cling to it.

Preheat your oven to 350°F (180°C).

Meanwhile, cook the pasta in lots of boiling salted water.

To make the sauce, melt the butter in a saucepan over medium heat. Add the garlic and stir for several minutes until it softens and flavours the butter. Add the flour and stir with a wooden spoon until a smooth paste forms (the roux). Combining the butter and flour into a roux first helps evenly distribute the flour throughout the sauce and prevents lumps.

Continue cooking a few more minutes as the roux toasts and develops a bit of flavour. Slowly stir in the wine and continue stirring until the mixture is smooth again.

Add both milks and switch to a whisk, mixing until the sauce is smooth again. Continue whisking until the mixture is very thick, a few minutes longer.

Stir in the cheese, Dijon mustard, paprika, cayenne pepper and salt. Stir the cooked pasta into the cheese mixture. Pour everything into a 9- × 13-inch (3.5 L) ovenproof casserole or baking dish.

Toss the bread with a splash or two of olive oil, then sprinkle it evenly over the top of the cheese mixture. Bake until it is heated through and the bread topping is golden brown, about 30 minutes.

FETTUCCINE ALFREDO

This classic dish is elegantly tasty, simple and super speedy. The creamy, cheesy sauce that makes Fettuccine Alfredo so memorable easily forms when great Parmesan cheese and a splash of cream are simply tossed together with hot noodles and aromatics. This dish is at its best when you make it and serve it immediately. SERVES 4

one 1 lb (454 g) package of fettuccine
½ stick (¼ cup/60 mL) of butter
2 cloves of garlic, minced
1 cup (250 mL) of heavy cream (35%)
1 cup (250 mL) or more of
   freshly grated Grana Padano
   Parmesan cheese

¼ teaspoon (1 mL) of freshly
   ground nutmeg
a sprinkle or two of sea salt and
   freshly ground pepper
½ cup (125 mL) of minced parsley
½ cup (125 mL) of minced chives
   or sliced green onions
lots of freshly ground pepper

Cook the fettuccine in lots of boiling salted water. (See Cooking Pasta, page 158.)

Meanwhile, in a separate saucepan, melt the butter over medium heat. Add the garlic and gently sauté until it softens and flavours the butter.

Add the cream and bring to a simmer. Stir in the cheese, nutmeg and salt and pepper and heat through.

Toss in the cooked pasta along with the parsley, chives or green onions. Season with lots of freshly ground pepper. Toss well to combine everything, and serve immediately.

freestyle VARIATION

There are many ingredients that may be added to this pasta to round out your meal and add a signature twist. Try thinly sliced basil leaves, a grilled and sliced chicken breast, pan-seared scallops, diced sun-dried tomatoes, pitted black olives, or steamed broccoli, frozen peas or any other vegetable.

SPAGHETTI WITH HIDDEN-VEGETABLE TOMATO SAUCE

Sometimes what you don't know can help you, especially when it comes to getting vegetables on the table. Kids will always eat pasta with tomato sauce but they won't always eat their vegetables—so it can help to magically, mysteriously hide them in the sauce. This is the sort of sauce that you may end up making on a regular basis, so it's worth investing in an immersion blender. It really speeds up the works. SERVES 4

2 tablespoons (30 mL) of olive oil
2 onions, peeled and chopped
4 cloves of garlic, minced
one 28 oz (796 mL) can of whole
　　tomatoes
a sprinkle or two of sea salt
　　and freshly ground pepper

1 teaspoon (5 mL) of dried oregano
2 carrots, peeled and shredded
1 bell pepper, any colour, chopped
1 zucchini, shredded
a few handfuls of baby spinach

Heat the oil in a saucepan with the onions and garlic. Sauté them until they begin to soften and caramelize. Pour in the tomatoes, toss in the salt and pepper, oregano, carrots, bell pepper and zucchini. Simmer for 20 minutes or so.

Stir in the spinach and continue simmering briefly as it wilts and heats through.

Purée the sauce with an immersion blender directly in the pot to minimize mess or with your food processor or blender. Reheat as needed, then cross your fingers and serve with your family's favourite pasta.

freestyle VARIATION

Just about any vegetable can be simmered until soft and then puréed into this sauce. Green vegetables will darken the colour a bit and might not impress some critics. Broccoli, fennel, even sweet potato can be grated in. For green-loving eaters, the baby spinach leaves may be brought out of hiding, kept whole and simply tossed with the hot sauce and the freshly cooked pasta. Instead of whole canned tomatoes (which are only cooked in the can), you may use the less-flavourful puréed, crushed or diced canned tomatoes (which are all cooked out of the can first and then a second time in the can).

SPAGHETTI & MEATBALLS
WITH SIMPLE TOMATO SAUCE

There's nothing more satisfying than a bowl full of spaghetti and meatballs and my gold standard tomato sauce. Every cook has an all-purpose tomato sauce up his or her sleeve, a perfect last-minute pasta sauce that's just as good served without meatballs. SERVES 4 TO 6

SIMPLE TOMATO SAUCE
a splash of olive oil
1 large onion, minced
1 whole head of garlic cloves, peeled
one 28 oz (796 mL) can
    of whole tomatoes
1 teaspoon (5 mL) of dried oregano
1 bay leaf
a sprinkle or two of sea salt
    and freshly ground pepper

MEATBALLS
½ cup (125 mL) of breadcrumbs
½ cup (125 mL) of milk

1 lb (500 g) of ground beef
1 onion, peeled and grated
2 cloves of garlic, finely minced
½ cup (125 mL) of grated
    Parmesan cheese
1 egg
a bunch of chopped parsley
½ teaspoon (2 mL) of ground nutmeg
1 tablespoon (15 mL) of dried oregano
a sprinkle or two of sea salt and freshly
    ground pepper
a few splashes of olive oil
spaghetti

freestyle VARIATION

There are lots of secret ingredients, like the nutmeg or oregano, that you can add to your meatballs to add personalized flavour. Try a spoonful of dried thyme, Worcestershire sauce or soy sauce.

Make the tomato sauce first so it will be ready when you need it. Begin by splashing some olive oil into a small saucepan over medium-high heat. Add the onion and garlic and sauté until they just begin to turn golden brown, about 5 minutes. Add the tomatoes, oregano, bay leaf and salt and pepper and bring to a simmer. Continue simmering for 15 minutes or so.

Purée the sauce with an immersion blender, or, for a more rustic texture, mash the tomatoes with the back of a spoon.

Meanwhile, make the meatballs. Toss the breadcrumbs into a small bowl and pour the milk over them. Stir to combine and set the mixture aside until the crumbs have absorbed all the milk. The breadcrumbs will help absorb and hold onto the moisture, which is the key to a perfect meatball.

Place the ground beef into a large mixing bowl and add the onion, garlic, Parmesan and egg. Add the breadcrumb mixture and parsley. Season with nutmeg, oregano and salt and pepper. Mix well with your hands and form 12 meatballs.

Preheat a large, heavy skillet over medium-high heat. When it's hot, add a splash of olive oil, enough to cover the bottom with a thin film. Carefully add the meatballs. Patiently sear them, turning them until they are browned well on all sides. Drain off any excess fat. Add the simple tomato sauce, cover the pan, turn down the heat and simmer until the meatballs are cooked through, about 15 minutes.

Meanwhile, cook a batch of spaghetti in lots of boiling salted water. (See Cooking Pasta, page 158.) Drain without rinsing, and serve with meatballs overtop.

LASAGNA WITH SPEEDY MEAT SAUCE

The best lasagna is made with two different sauces: a tomato sauce and a cheese sauce. It's the sort of dish that's worth taking the time to make right, but that doesn't mean you have to slave away in the kitchen for hours. SERVES 6

MEAT SAUCE

a few splashes of olive oil

2 onions, chopped

1 whole head of garlic cloves, minced

1 lb (500 g) of ground beef

4 Italian sausages (casings removed)

one 28 oz (796 mL) can of crushed or puréed tomatoes

1 cup (250 mL) of beef or chicken broth (homemade or canned— see page 24 for Homemade Chicken Broth)

2 tablespoons (30 mL) of dried oregano

2 bay leaves

a sprinkle or two of sea salt and freshly ground pepper

CHEESE SAUCE

2 eggs, whisked together

4 cups (1 L) of shredded mozzarella cheese

one 1 lb (495 g) carton of ricotta cheese

1 cup (250 mL) of grated Parmesan cheese

½ cup (125 mL) of heavy cream (35%)

a sprinkle or two of sea salt and freshly ground pepper

LASAGNA

one 1 lb (454 g) box of ready-to-bake lasagna noodles

1 cup (250 mL) of grated Parmesan cheese

1 cup (250 mL) of shredded mozzarella cheese

For the meat sauce, begin by splashing some olive oil into a large saucepan over medium-high heat. Add the onions and garlic and sauté just until they soften and begin to brown, about 5 minutes.

Add the ground beef and sausage meat. Use a wooden spoon to break the meats up into very small pieces. Add the tomatoes and their juice, beef or chicken broth, oregano, bay leaves and salt and pepper. Stir well and continue heating until the entire mixture is simmering and heated through. It's ready for the lasagna as soon as it heats through. By not browning the meat, it stays tender without a long simmering time and adds a rich meaty flavour. Taste the sauce and add more salt and pepper if you like.

To make the cheese sauce, mix together the whisked eggs, the mozzarella, ricotta and Parmesan cheeses and the cream. Season with salt and pepper.

Preheat your oven to 375°F (190°C). Lightly oil a 9- × 13-inch (3.5 L) baking pan. To assemble the lasagna, layer the ingredients in the pan in this order: 2 cups (500 mL) or so of the meat sauce, a layer of noodles, one-third of the cheese sauce, one-third of the Parmesan cheese, another noodle layer, another meat sauce layer, another noodle layer, one-third of the cheese sauce, one-third of the Parmesan, another noodle layer, the remaining meat sauce, the remaining cheese sauce and the mozzarella and remaining Parmesan.

Cover the pan tightly with foil and bake for 1 hour. Remove the foil and bake for another 15 minutes, giving the top a chance to get golden brown.

FARFALLE WITH ROASTED TOMATO GARLIC SAUCE

You haven't lived until you've roasted tomatoes with onions and garlic and tossed them with pasta! Roasting reveals a deep, satisfying flavour hidden in tomatoes. This will become one of your favourite ways to dress up pasta. My family loves the simple rustic flavours of this dish, and I'm sure yours will too. SERVES 4

a dozen or so plum tomatoes,
   halved lengthwise
2 onions, diced
1 head of whole garlic cloves, peeled

a generous splash of olive oil
a sprinkle or two of sea salt and
   freshly ground pepper
one 1 lb (454 g) box of farfalle

You can use any of your favourite pastas for this dish. For lots of bright flavour bursts, try tossing the tomatoes with a spoonful of fennel seeds before roasting them or adding lots of whole basil leaves just before serving.

Preheat your oven to 375°F (190°C).

Toss the tomatoes, onions, garlic and olive oil together. Season the works with salt and pepper, and then toss everything into a 9- × 13-inch (3.5 L) casserole or other baking dish.

Roast until the tomatoes shrivel and begin to brown a bit, about 1 hour or so. As they roast, their flavours will concentrate and caramelize. The heat will also break them down a bit so they'll form a loose sauce when they're tossed with the pasta.

When the tomatoes are done roasting, discard any onion slices that may have blackened a bit—a small price to pay for the rich flavours of roasted tomato!

Cook the pasta in lots of boiling salted water. (See Cooking Pasta, page 158.) Toss the hot pasta with the hot sauce and enjoy the tasty, roasted tomatoes and mellow, whole garlic cloves.

PENNE WITH RED PEPPER SAUCE & SPINACH

Tomatoes aren't the only sweet red fruit that make great pasta sauce. Red bell peppers are excellent too, especially paired with the faint licorice flavour of fennel seeds. SERVES 4

4 red bell peppers, halved, seeded and
    roughly chopped
2 large onions, roughly chopped
1 whole head of garlic cloves, peeled
¼ cup (60 mL) of olive oil

2 tablespoons (30 mL) of fennel seeds
a sprinkle or two of sea salt and freshly
    ground pepper
one 1 lb (454 g) box of penne
a few handfuls of baby spinach

Preheat oven to 350°F (180°C).

Toss the peppers, onion, garlic, olive oil, fennel seed and salt and pepper together in a large bowl until thoroughly coated. Pour into a 9- × 13-inch (3.5 L) baking pan. Roast until peppers are softened and caramelized, about 1 hour.

Transfer the roasted vegetables into a medium saucepan and purée with an immersion blender, adding a splash of water to help it along. Alternatively, put into a food processor or blender and purée until smooth. Taste and add more salt and pepper to taste.

Just prior to serving, reheat the sauce in a large pot.

Cook the pasta in lots of boiling salted water. (See Cooking Pasta, page 158.) Toss the hot pasta with the reheated red pepper sauce and the baby spinach and serve immediately.

You may use any of your favourite pastas for this dish. As you reheat the sauce, add in chopped fresh oregano or thyme.

PENNE WITH TOMATO BACON SAUCE

This is the pasta sauce I crave more than any other. It's easy to make and perfect when there's a finicky eater at the table because the bacon is irresistible. You can combine the simple flavours of a great tomato sauce with crowd-pleasing bacon, and you're guaranteed a winner. SERVES 4

8 slices of bacon, chopped
1 onion, finely chopped
8 cloves of garlic, thinly sliced
one 28 oz (796 mL) can
    of crushed tomatoes

1 tablespoon (15 mL) of fresh thyme,
    rosemary or oregano
a sprinkle or two of sea salt and freshly
    ground pepper
one 1 lb (454 g) box of penne

Freestyle VARIATION

You can use any type of pasta and any type of canned tomatoes for this sauce. If you choose whole tomatoes, purée them before you add them to the sauce. For a decadent treat and a richer flavour, you can leave all of the bacon fat in the pot. If you don't have any fresh herbs, 1 teaspoon (5 mL) of dried oregano, rosemary or thyme will work well too.

Toss the bacon into a large saucepan over medium-high heat. Add a splash of water. Cook until the water evaporates and the bacon begins to brown. Continue stirring, lowering the heat a notch, until the bacon is crispy and brown. Drain away most (or some) of its fat, leaving enough behind to sauté the vegetables.

Add the onion and garlic and cook until they soften and begin to caramelize. Pour in the tomatoes, rinsing out the can with a splash of water and adding that too. Sprinkle in the herb of your choice and season with salt and pepper. Simmer for 20 minutes or so.

Cook penne in lots of boiling salted water. (See Cooking Pasta, page 158.) Toss with the sauce and enjoy!

PENNE WITH SMOKED SALMON & CREAM CHEESE SAUCE

This is my family's all-time favourite dinner party pasta dish. Our friends request it all the time. I'm happy to oblige because it tastes great, and the sauce makes itself! It's easy. Steaming wet, just-cooked pasta and melting cream cheese form an incredibly smooth luxurious sauce. The smoked salmon adds flavour extravagance that's balanced by the familiar flavours of capers, dill, lemon, onion and mustard. A five-star dish for sharing! SERVES 4

one 1 lb (454 g) box of penne
1 cup (250 mL) of cream cheese,
    softened
1 bunch of fresh dill, chopped
4 green onions, thinly sliced
zest and juice of 1 lemon

1 tablespoon (15 mL) of Dijon mustard
¼ cup (60 mL) of capers
8 oz (250 g) of smoked salmon
    or more, cut into ribbons
a sprinkle or two of sea salt and freshly
    ground pepper

Cook penne in lots of boiling salted water until al dente—cooked through and tender but still retaining some texture and chew.

Scoop out some of the starchy cooking water and reserve. Drain the pasta but not quite all the way. Leave it a bit wet. Put the pasta back into the pot along with a splash or two of the reserved water.

While the pasta is still steaming hot, immediately add the cream cheese, dill, green onions, lemon zest and juice, mustard and capers. Stir with a wooden spoon as the cheese melts and forms a creamy sauce.

At the last second briefly stir in the smoked salmon; this way it won't break up as much. Season with salt and pepper and serve immediately.

You can use any of your favourite shaped pastas for this dish, like bowties; but ribbon pastas, like spaghetti, don't work as well. This dish also works equally well with any kind of smoked fish. And if you don't have green onions, try a finely minced red onion. If you don't have capers, try a spoonful of standard green hotdog relish.

PASTA WITH BRAISED CHICKEN, SAUSAGES, PEPPERS & TOMATOES

This rustic dish shows how easy it is to braise any type of meat in a tomato sauce. The results are tender, flavourful and perfect for any type of pasta. This is a hearty meal in a bowl. SERVES 4

a few splashes of olive oil
6 chicken thighs (skin-on and bone-in)
4 Italian sausages
2 large onions, diced
1 head of whole garlic cloves, peeled
1 red bell pepper, diced
1 green bell pepper, diced

1 cup (250 mL) of your favourite red wine
one 28 oz (796 mL) can of tomatoes
1 teaspoon (5 mL) of dried oregano
2 bay leaves
a sprinkle or two of sea salt and freshly ground pepper
one 1 lb (454 g) box of your favourite pasta

Splash enough olive oil into a large sauce pot to cover the bottom with a thin film. Begin heating over medium-high heat.

Pat the chicken thighs dry with paper towels. Carefully add them to the pot, skin side down. If there is still room, add the sausages. Patiently brown the chicken and sausages on both sides. When they are golden brown and beautiful, remove them from the pan and set aside on a plate.

Drain some of the fat from the pan and put it back on the heat. Add the onions and stir for a few minutes until their moisture dissolves any lingering brown bits on the bottom of the pan. When the onions begin to caramelize and turn golden brown, add the garlic. Continue cooking for a few minutes longer.

Return the chicken and sausages to the pan and then toss in the bell peppers. Pour in the wine and tomatoes and add the oregano and bay leaves. Season to taste with salt and pepper. Bring to a boil, then lower the heat just enough to maintain a simmer. Cover with a tight-fitting lid, and continue simmering until the chicken is cooked through and tender, about 1 hour or so.

When you are almost ready to serve, cook the pasta in lots of boiling salted water. (See Cooking Pasta, page 158.) Drain the pasta and pour into a large festive bowl, ladle the sauce over the pasta and serve immediately!

You may use any cut of chicken or type of sausage to make this dish. Beef short ribs work well too. Try adding a head of chopped fennel to the sauce along with the peppers.

GRAINS, POTATOES & BEANS

BARLEY RISOTTO WITH BACON

This is one of my all-time favourite comfort foods. Just like high-starch rice, barley may be simmered and stirred into a smooth, creamy risotto, absorbing the flavour of the bacon and rich chicken broth as it cooks slowly. The results are richly flavoured and deeply satisfying. SERVES 4 AS A MAIN COURSE, 6 TO 8 AS A SIDE DISH

8 cups (2 L) or so of chicken broth (see
    page 24 for homemade)
8 slices of bacon, thinly chopped
2 or 3 onions, peeled and chopped
4 or 5 cloves of garlic, minced
1 cup (250 mL) of pearl barley
½ cup (125 mL) of white wine

a sprinkle or two of sea salt and freshly
    ground pepper
2 tablespoons (30 mL) of chopped
    fresh thyme
1 cup (250 mL) of grated Grana
    Padano Parmesan cheese

Pour the chicken broth into a stockpot and bring to a very slow simmer over medium heat.

Meanwhile, in another saucepan, fry the bacon over medium-high heat until it is crisp and golden brown. Pour off about half of the fat. Add the onions and garlic and sauté them for a few minutes until they're translucent and soft.

Stir in the barley and continue cooking, stirring constantly until the grains are well coated with oil and slightly toasted, about 3 minutes.

Lower the heat, pour in the wine and continue stirring as the barley quickly absorbs the liquid. Begin adding the heated stock, 1 cup (250 mL) or so at a time, stirring constantly to allow each addition of the liquid to be absorbed by the barley before adding more.

> Because the broth is already hot, the temperature of the barley will stay consistently hot, which, along with the constant stirring, encourages the release of the starch in the barley. In turn, the starch thickens the surrounding liquid and makes it creamy.

Continue stirring in the hot broth until the risotto is tender and creamy. If you run out of broth, switch to hot water. Taste frequently to judge the doneness of the barley grains. It will take about 45 minutes from the time you add the first broth until the rice is done.

Season with salt and pepper and stir in the thyme and cheese. Serve immediately.

Try adding a handful of your favourite herb instead of the thyme. Chives, green onions, parsley and rosemary all work well. If you run out of broth, you may use simmering hot water. This risotto-style cooking method is also great vegetarian style, without the bacon and the chicken broth.

RICE PILAF WITH ALMONDS & APRICOTS

This simple, versatile rice pilaf is distinguished by its method—sautéing the grains briefly in oil or butter before adding liquid—which adds flavour and helps the grains stay fluffy and separate. Rice pilaf is also a great jumping-off point for freestyle flavouring. SERVES 4 TO 6

2 tablespoons (30 mL) of butter
1 or 2 onions, chopped
1 cup (250 mL) of any white rice
1 bay leaf
½ cup (125 mL) of slivered almonds

½ cup (125 mL) of sliced dried apricots
2 cups (500 mL) of water or chicken
  broth (see page 24 for homemade)
a sprinkle or two of sea salt and freshly
  ground pepper

Melt the butter in a saucepan over medium heat. Add the onions and sauté for a few minutes until they just begin to turn golden.

Add the rice and continue cooking and stirring until the grains are well coated with the butter.

Add the bay leaf, almonds and apricots. Pour in the water or broth and bring to a boil. Season with salt and pepper. Stir briefly, cover and cook over a low heat until the rice is tender and has absorbed all the liquid, about 15 minutes.

Turn off the heat, and without removing the lid let the rice rest for 5 minutes or so before serving.

You may stir in a spoonful or so of any of your favourite herbs. Tarragon, thyme and rosemary are all excellent choices. You may use brown rice as well; just add another ½ cup (125 mL) of water and increase the simmering time to 45 minutes. For an extra special touch, try adding a pinch of saffron with the rice.

RISOTTO WITH PARMESAN & PEAS

Risotto is one of the world's great rice dishes. It's a traditional Italian dish that must be made from rice varieties with very high starch contents. Its distinctive cooking method gently coaxes the starches out of each rice grain, giving the dish its characteristic creaminess. An exercise in patience, but the results are more than worth the effort! SERVES 4 AS A MAIN COURSE, 6 AS A SIDE DISH

8 or 9 cups (2 L) of chicken broth (see page 24 for homemade)
2 tablespoons (30 mL) of olive oil
2 onions, minced
4 cloves of garlic, minced
2 cups (500 mL) of Arborio, Carnaroli or other risotto-grade rice
½ cup (125 mL) of white wine

a sprinkle or two of sea salt and freshly ground pepper
1 cup (250 mL) of frozen peas
1 bunch of parsley, chopped
1 cup (250 mL) of grated Grana Padano Parmesan cheese

Freestyle VARIATION

There are as many different types of risotto as there are Italian cooks, and each has a signature ingredient or two. Feel free to add olives, artichokes, sun-dried tomatoes and mushrooms. You may finish the risotto by stirring in lots of fresh Basil Pesto (page 246) or any other fresh herb, such as thyme, chives or oregano.

Pour the chicken broth into a stockpot, and bring to a very slow simmer over medium heat.

Meanwhile, splash the olive oil into a second saucepan over medium heat. Add the onions and garlic and sauté them for a few minutes until they're translucent and soft. Stir in the rice and continue cooking, stirring constantly until the grains are well coated with oil and slightly toasted, about 3 minutes. Keep an eye on the rice grains; they'll transform from pure white to almost entirely opaque.

Pour in the wine and stir because the rice quickly absorbs the liquid. Begin adding the heated stock, 1 cup (250 mL) at a time, stirring constantly to allow each addition of the liquid to be absorbed by the rice before adding more.

Because the broth is already hot, the temperature of the rice will stay consistently hot, which, along with the constant stirring, encourages the release of the starch in the rice. In turn, the starch thickens the surrounding liquid and makes it creamy.

Continue adding the hot broth, stirring frequently, until the risotto is tender and creamy. Taste frequently to judge the doneness of the rice grains. It will take about 20 minutes from the time you add the first broth to when the rice is done.

Season with salt and pepper, then stir in the peas, parsley and cheese. Serve immediately.

BROWN BUTTER MASHED POTATOES

There are as many ways to flavour mashed potatoes as there are cooks. These are my gold standard. They're simple, with a twist: brown butter. You won't believe how much flavour is locked into a stick of butter, but you will believe these are the best mashed spuds you've ever had. SERVES 4

2 lb (1 kg) of potatoes (unpeeled)
   (about 4 large)
1 stick (½ cup/125 mL) of butter
½ cup (125 mL) milk

a few pinches of nutmeg
a sprinkle or two of sea salt
   and freshly ground pepper

Cut the potatoes into large chunks and steam, boil or microwave them until they're tender. Drain well.

Place a saucepan over medium heat. Add the butter and begin heating and melting it. Keep a close eye on it as it foams. Swirl it gently, watching the colour. When it turns a deep golden brown and releases the aroma of toasting nuts, immediately pour in the milk to lower its temperature and stop it from browning further. Bring to a simmer.

Once the potatoes are tender, mash in the brown butter and milk, nutmeg and salt and pepper. Taste and season a bit more if needed. Then watch the bowl empty!

Because butter contains as much as 20 percent water, it will begin to steam and foam. Once the water has evaporated, the foam will subside, and the butter's temperature will begin to rise past the boiling point of water. The milk fat solids that are 1 or 2 percent of the butter will then begin to brown.

You can mash any potato, but your best bets are the low-moisture, high-starch varieties that are also the best for baking. My favourite is the Yukon Gold. Its creamy texture and golden colour are perfect with the brown butter. You can peel the potatoes if you prefer but you'll lose some rustic flavour and some nutrients if you do. Your choice! Sliced green onions, chives and chopped parsley add both flavour and colour. French chefs always add a pinch of elegant nutmeg to their potato purées. It adds a pleasing mysterious flavour but feel free to leave it out.

OVEN-CRISPED POTATOES

If you like golden brown crispy crusty potatoes, then this dish is for you.
It was originally created as a way to use up leftover boiled or baked potatoes,
but it's so good that you'll soon be cooking potatoes just so you can smash
and crisp 'em.

FOR EACH PERSON YOU'LL NEED
1 leftover baked or boiled skin-on
   potato

1 tablespoon (15 mL) of oil
   for each potato
a sprinkle or two of sea salt and freshly
   ground pepper for each potato

freestyle VARIATION

If you don't have any leftover potatoes, simply bake a few until tender
in a 400°F (200°C) oven. Alternatively, steam or microwave them.
For any freshly cooked potato, it's
best if you cool it first. A cool potato
doesn't crumble as much when it's
smashed; it tends to stay together in
one big smashed piece. Along with
the salt and pepper, try sprinkling
whole fennel seeds over the potatoes. You'll love their soft chewy
texture and delicate licorice-like
flavour.

Preheat your oven to 450°F (230°C).

Place the cooked potatoes on a lightly oiled rimmed baking sheet. Push
down on each potato with a small flat plate until the potato smashes and
spreads out to about twice its original size. You may also use a potato masher
if you have one. If a few pieces get loose just push them back into the rest of
the works.

Brush or drizzle each potato with 1 tablespoon (15 mL) of oil, then season
with salt and pepper. Bake until the exposed potato flesh transform into a
crispy golden masterpiece, about 30 to 40 minutes.

HERB-ROASTED POTATOES

The secret to perfectly oven-roasted potatoes is a two-step process. First, gently boil and cook potatoes through, then rapidly roast and brown them. The resulting crisp exterior and tender interior are quite addictive. SERVES 4

1 lb (500 g) of any potato, large or
  small (unpeeled)
¼ cup (60 mL) of olive oil
a sprinkle or two of thyme or
  rosemary, dried or fresh

a sprinkle or two of sea salt and freshly
  ground pepper
chopped parsley and/or a few sliced
  green onions, for serving

Cover the potatoes with salted water and bring to a simmer, cooking just until tender. Alternatively steam the potatoes until they're just tender.

When they are cool enough to handle, cut them into large bite-sized chunks. Depending on the size of the potato, this may mean simply cutting a smaller one in half or a larger one into 6 or 8 pieces.

Meanwhile, place a baking pan, casserole dish or large skillet in your oven and preheat it to 375°F (190°C). When the potatoes are done, toss them with the olive oil, thyme or rosemary and salt and pepper, coating each piece evenly.

Carefully add them to the preheated pan. The heat of the pan will help keep them from sticking.

Roast until golden brown and crunchy, about 30 minutes or so. Stir occasionally to help them brown evenly.

Just before serving toss with the parsley or green onions or both.

Try tossing the freshly roasted potatoes with a few handfuls of baby spinach.

TWICE-BAKED POTATOES

A baked stuffed potato is a thing of beauty. It's the perfect blend of all your favourite potato topping flavours mixed together in an easy-to-make, easy-to-serve, all-in-one package. SERVES 4

4 large baking potatoes (unpeeled)
4 slices of fried, crispy bacon
1 cup (250 mL) of shredded
　　cheddar cheese

4 green onions, sliced
a sprinkle or two of sea salt and
　　freshly ground pepper

You may stir any of your favourite potato toppings into the mix. Try sour cream, horseradish, fresh herbs like chives and parsley, nutmeg, any cheese, smoked salmon, ham, left-over chicken . . . The sky is the limit!

Bake the potatoes for 45 minutes or so at 400°F (200°C) until they are tender when pierced with a fork. Let them rest until they are cool enough to handle.

Slice the top off each potato, lengthwise, and scoop the flesh out into a mixing bowl.

Chop the bacon and stir in with the cheddar cheese, green onion and salt and pepper. Mash well to combine everything and then evenly stuff the mixture back into the potato shells.

Place on a baking sheet and bake until the potatoes heat through and the cheese melts and begins to brown, 20 minutes or so.

MAPLE BAKED BEANS

Beans have the wonderful ability to absorb lots of flavour while they slowly bake. They're nutritious, easy and, most of all, tasty—especially when they bake with maple and bacon. SERVES 4 TO 6

2 cups (500 mL) of dried navy
    or white beans, soaked in lots
    of cold water overnight
2 cups (500 mL) of water
1 cup (250 mL) of maple syrup
6 slices of thick-cut fried bacon,
    diced, fat reserved
1 or 2 large onions, peeled and diced

1 tablespoon (15 mL) of powdered
    ginger
2 tablespoons (30 mL) of any mustard
a dash or two of Worcestershire sauce
a sprinkle or two of sea salt and freshly
    ground pepper
1 tablespoon (15 mL) of any vinegar

Preheat your oven to 300°F (150°C).

Strain the beans out of their soaking water and give them a good rinse. No nutrients are lost in the soaking and rinsing; instead, the beans rehydrate, which will speed up their cooking time.

Toss the beans into a saucepan and cover them with cold water. Bring to a boil and then reduce the heat and simmer until the beans are tender, about 45 minutes.

Drain the beans and place them in a 4-quart (4 L) ovenproof baking dish with a tight-fitting lid. Add the maple syrup, bacon, onions, ginger, mustard, Worcestershire sauce and salt and pepper. Add as much or as little of the reserved bacon fat as you care to.

Cover and place in the oven and bake until the beans have absorbed most of the liquid and are tender, about 1 hour or so.

Stir in the vinegar just before serving.

Try adding a spoonful or so of your favourite chopped fresh herb. Rosemary and thyme work very well. You can also use a spoonful or so of chili powder or curry powder.

POTATO BACON CHEDDAR TART

I've been making this dish for a long time. It's a bit involved but it remains one of the most impressive potato dishes I know. This special occasion treat features the classic trio of potatoes, bacon and cheddar. It takes a while to make, but the results are more than worth it. It's the sort of thing that looks complicated until you try it and quickly realize how simple it is to master. SERVES 8

2 lb (1 kg) of room-temperature bacon
lots of freshly ground pepper
4 cups (1 L) of shredded aged cheddar
5 or 6 large baking potatoes
    (unpeeled)

a sprinkle or two of sea salt and freshly
    ground pepper
1 onion, minced
4 cloves of garlic, minced

Try mixing a few spoonfuls of your favourite fresh herb into the onion mixture. Thyme, rosemary and tarragon all work well.

Preheat your oven to 350°F (180°C).

Carefully arrange the bacon in a radial pattern from the centre of the bottom of a 10- or 12-inch (25 or 30 cm) round non-stick baking pan; arrange the bacon so that it fits along the bottom of the pan, continuing up and over the sides. Let the ends hang over. The slices should overlap slightly around the sides of the pan. To reduce the thickness of the bacon in the centre, stagger every other piece, starting it 2 inches (5 cm) from the centre and extending it further than the adjacent slices.

With the palm of your hand, flatten the centre area, leaving no gaps in the bacon. Season the bacon with lots of pepper and then sprinkle on several spoonfuls of the shredded cheddar.

Kitchen specialty stores carry a French slicing tool known as a mandoline. It's a fancy chef tool but easily slices the potatoes into even rounds. It's not absolutely necessary though—a sharp knife works well too!

Slice the potatoes as thinly and uniformly as you can, about 1/4 inch (6 mm) thick.

Arrange a circular pattern of overlapping slices around the inside bottom edge of the pan. Continue arranging overlapping layers of the potatoes until the bottom is evenly covered. Season the potatoes with salt and pepper.

Mix together the onion and garlic and sprinkle some of the mixture onto the potatoes. Continue with a layer of the shredded cheese. Cover with another layer of the potato, pressing it down firmly before continuing with alternate layers of the potatoes, onion mixture and cheese, insetting each a bit from the edge of the pan until the top is 1 inch (2.5 cm) or so higher than the pan's rim. Fold the overhanging bacon neatly up and over the top of the potatoes.

Trim a small piece of parchment paper and place it in between an ovenproof lid and the bacon. This will prevent the bacons ends from pulling back and shrinking during cooking.

Place the pan on a baking sheet and bake for at least 2½ to 3 hours. You'll know it's done when a small, thin bladed knife inserts easily.

Pour off as much of the fat as possible. Let the tart stand for 15 minutes and then invert it onto a cutting surface. Slice into wedges and serve immediately.

POLENTA

A bowl full of freshly made corn polenta is one of the world's great grain dishes. Polenta is a traditional Italian pudding made with cornmeal. Freshly made, it has a soft, creamy texture, and it is addictively delicious. It can also be served by cooling and hardening it, then slicing it and grilling or pan-searing it until it forms a beautiful crispy crust with a creamy interior. SERVES 4 TO 6

a splash of vegetable oil
1 or 2 onions, chopped
a few cloves of garlic, minced
2 cups (500 mL) of milk
2 cups (500 mL) of chicken broth (see
    page 24 for homemade) or 2 more
    cups (500 mL) of milk

1 cup (250 mL) of coarse
    yellow cornmeal
1 cup (250 mL) of frozen corn
½ cup (125 mL) of grated Grana
    Padano Parmesan cheese
    or shredded cheddar cheese
a sprinkle or two of sea salt
    and freshly ground pepper

Splash the vegetable oil in a large saucepan over a medium heat. Add the onions and garlic and sauté, stirring, until they just begin to turn golden brown, about 5 minutes.

Add the milk and broth and bring everything to a simmer. Add the cornmeal in a slow steady stream, whisking constantly to prevent lumping. Switch to a wooden spoon as soon as all the cornmeal is in the broth. The cornmeal will quickly thicken beyond the usefulness of a whisk.

Lower the heat and continue cooking, stirring frequently, until the mixture really thickens, 15 minutes or so.

Stir in the frozen corn, cheese and salt and pepper and serve immediately with lots of melted butter while the polenta is still soft and creamy. Alternatively, preheat your oven to 350°F (180°C) and pour the polenta into a loaf pan or baking dish. Bake for 15 minutes and refrigerate until firm.

To reheat, cut the polenta into thick slices and grill them. You may also toss the slices with more cornmeal and pan-fry them.

Smooth polenta takes patience because you have to wait for the corn granules to swell and soften. In this recipe there are 4 parts of liquid for every 1 part cornmeal. The liquid will thicken faster if you add more cornmeal—a 3-to-1 ratio—but the finished texture will be a bit coarse. For a more refined, even smoother polenta, you may continue stirring for up to 30 minutes before adding the finishing ingredients. For a lighter polenta, you may substitute water for some or all of the milk or chicken broth.

For more flavour, stir in 1 cup (250 mL) or so of aged cheddar cheese and some crisp bacon bits. You may also stir in a few spoonfuls of pesto (see page 246 for Basil Pesto) or lots of your favourite chopped herb.

GREENS & GARDEN VEGETABLES

APPLE STEWED RED CABBAGE

Apples and red cabbage were made for each other! This is a traditional side dish for just about any meat, poultry, pork or game. The earthy bitterness of the cabbage is perfectly balanced by the sweetness of the apple and the sourness of the vinegar. SERVES 4

a splash or two of vegetable oil
1 or 2 onions, peeled and sliced
3 or 4 cloves of garlic, thinly sliced
1 head of red cabbage, thinly sliced
2 or 3 of your favourite apples,
   cored and chopped

2 tablespoons (30 mL) of honey
a few splashes of cider vinegar
a few splashes of cider, apple
   juice or water
a sprinkle or two of sea salt
   and freshly ground pepper

Freestyle VARIATION

For a more traditional, richer flavour, begin with 3 or 4 slices of fried chopped bacon before sautéing the onions. For an even more traditional flavour, try adding ½ teaspoon (2 mL) of caraway seeds with the apples. For extra texture and appearance, try reserving some of the apples and stirring them in at the last minute. The first ones dissolve as they cook; the second ones will stay whole.

Splash the vegetable oil into a heavy saucepan over medium heat. Add the onions and sauté until they're golden brown. Add the garlic and continue cooking for another minute or so. Add the cabbage, apples, honey, cider vinegar and the cider (or apple juice or water). Season with salt and pepper.

Bring everything to a simmer and then lower the heat just enough to maintain the simmer. Cover with a tight-fitting lid and continue cooking until the cabbage is tender, about 30 minutes.

ASIAN GREENS WITH THREE SESAMES

A bowl full of warm Asian greens is one of the healthiest things you can put on your table. It's also one of the tastiest, especially if you simply steam the greens and toss them with a quick, warm sesame dressing. SERVES 4

1 lb (500 g) or more of any
   Asian greens
1 clove of garlic, sliced
¼ cup (60 mL) of tahini
   (sesame paste)

2 tablespoons (30 mL) of soy sauce
½ tsp (2 mL) dark (roasted) sesame oil
zest and juice of ½ lemon
2 tablespoons (30 mL) of sesame
   seeds

Rinse the greens well in lots of cold running water. Shake them dry.

Splash a ½ inch (1 cm) or so of water into a saucepan. Add the garlic and bring the mixture to a simmer for a moment or two, just long enough to take some of the pungent strength out of the garlic but not long enough to remove its aroma.

Add the rinsed greens, cover with a tight-fitting lid and continue steaming for a few minutes longer until the greens are tender.

Meanwhile, toss the tahini, soy sauce, dark sesame oil and lemon zest and juice into a salad bowl. Whisk them together and then add the just-steamed greens. Toss everything together and sprinkle on the sesame seeds.

There are many different Asian greens commonly available at your supermarket. Feel free to use any one of them or a mixture. Bok choy, yu choy, mizuna, tatsoi or pea shoots, even simple spinach, all work well.

BROWN BUTTER GREEN BEANS WITH TOASTED ALMONDS

Green beans are one of my favourite vegetables, especially when they're sprinkled with crunchy toasted nuts and dressed with brown butter. Browning butter is one of the all-time great flavour secrets; it's an easy way to unlock lots of hidden flavour and dress up your plate. Of course, for a healthier twist, you can simply use flavourful olive oil. SERVES 4

1 lb (500 g) of fresh green beans
2 tablespoons (30 mL) of butter
½ cup (125 mL) of sliced almonds
2 tablespoons (30 mL) of any vinegar

a sprinkle or two of sea salt and
   freshly ground pepper
a splash of water

Wash green beans and snip off the stem ends, leaving the beautiful curled tips.

Place a saucepan over medium heat. Add the butter and begin heating and melting it.

Keep a close eye on it as it foams. Swirl it gently, watching the colour. When it turns golden brown and releases the aroma of toasting nuts, immediately stir in the almonds to lower the butter's temperature and stop it from browning further.

Because butter contains as much as 20 percent water, it will begin to steam and foam. Once the water has evaporated, the foam will subside, and the butter's temperature will begin to rise past the boiling point of water. The milk fat solids that are 1 or 2 percent of the butter will then begin to brown.

Continue cooking, stirring the almonds as they heat through and gently toast. From the time the butter is added until the almonds are lightly browned will take about 5 minutes.

Add the green beans, vinegar and salt and pepper and a splash of water. Toss well to coat the beans with the butter and nuts. Cover the pan with a tight-fitting lid, lower the heat and continue cooking, steaming the beans until they're tender.

Try sprinkling in some of your favourite chopped fresh herb. Thyme, tarragon and green onions all work well. A single clove of thinly sliced garlic may also be added to the butter along with the nuts. For a special treat, try using pine nuts instead of almonds.

GARLIC SCENTED BROCCOLI

This is how most of the broccoli that lands on my table is cooked: scented with aromatic garlic as it gently steams. It's the quickest way I know to elegantly cook broccoli and show off its flavour and bright green nutritional value!

SERVES 4

1 head of broccoli
a splash of water
a splash of olive oil

1 or 2 cloves of garlic, thinly sliced
a sprinkle or two of sea salt and freshly
   ground pepper

Cut the broccoli into florets, discarding the tough stems.

Splash enough water into a small saucepan to cover the bottom about ¼ inch (6 mm) deep. Add the oil, garlic and salt and pepper and begin heating over medium-high heat. In a few moments the water will start to simmer, and the garlic will lose much of its pungency and perfume the steam.

Add the broccoli and cover the pot with a tight-fitting lid. Steam the broccoli until it is tender and bright green, no more than 5 minutes. The water should finish evaporating just as the broccoli finishes cooking.

Remove the pan from the heat, and give the pan a good shake. Serve immediately.

For an exotic flavour burst, splash in a bit of strongly flavoured sesame oil instead of the olive oil. You may also add a sprinkling of herbs for flavour along with the garlic.

GRILLED ASPARAGUS WITH PARSLEY PESTO

There are many ways to cook asparagus; my favourite is on the grill with lots of smoky flavour, especially when they're tossed with a batch of a quick and tasty variation of pesto. SERVES 4 TO 6

a large bunch of flat leaf parsley
½ cup (125 mL) of grated
   Parmesan cheese
½ cup (125 mL) of sliced almonds
a few splashes of your best olive oil
a sprinkle or two of sea salt
   and freshly ground pepper

1 or 2 bunches of fresh asparagus,
   woody ends trimmed
more splashes of your best olive oil
lots of sea salt and freshly
   ground pepper

Try adding a green onion or two to the pesto. You may use pine nuts instead of almonds.

For the pesto, simply purée the parsley, cheese, almonds and olive oil in your food processor until the mixture is smooth. Add just enough oil to help the mixture form a smooth purée; it's at its best somewhere between chunky and runny.

Taste it and season with salt and pepper. The pesto will keep in the refrigerator for a week or so.

Preheat your grill on its highest setting.

Toss the asparagus spears with a splash or two of olive oil and season them with lots of salt and pepper. Carefully place them on the hot grill, rotating them as they begin to cook. They're done when they're slightly charred and tender.

Arrange them on a serving platter and drizzle with lots of parsley pesto.

GRILLED VEGETABLES

Nothing tastes better than grilled vegetables. Nothing! These are one of the best ways I know to encourage mass vegetable consumption. The smoky charred aroma of your grill is always a crowd-pleaser. SERVES 4 TO 6

a few bell peppers, red, green or yellow
a zucchini or two
a yellow squash or two
an eggplant
a few large onions

a handful or two of asparagus,
    woody ends trimmed
a few splashes of olive oil
lots of sea salt and freshly
    ground pepper

Try tossing the just-grilled vegetables with a few handfuls of whole fresh basil leaves, a few spoonfuls of Basil Pesto (page 246) or black olive tapenade.

Preheat your grill to its highest setting.

Meanwhile, slice the bell peppers in half, then scoop out and discard their stems and seeds.

Trim the stem end off the zucchini and squash and cut them in half lengthwise.

Cut the eggplant into 3 or 4 lengthwise slices.

Peel the onion, then cut it into 3 or 4 thick slices, trying not to let the rings come apart.

Trim the woody ends of the asparagus.

Splash the vegetables with olive oil, and rub them by hand to coat them evenly. Take care not to undo the onion rings; they're much easier to handle if they stay nested. Season everything with lots of salt and pepper.

Carefully place the vegetables on your grill. Close the lid and wait a few minutes. When the vegetables begin to soften and char, flip them. Each vegetable will cook at its own pace so you'll need to keep an eye on things.

As the vegetables cook through, remove them from the grill. Stack them neatly on a cutting board, and cut them into smaller bite-sized pieces.

Toss everything together and serve immediately.

RATATOUILLE

Ratatouille is one of the world's great vegetable dishes. It's a brightly fla-voured rustic dish of stewed vegetables that traces its roots to the sunny south of France. It's simple to make—and simple to vary—and usually includes tomatoes, onions, garlic, peppers, eggplant and zucchini slowly cooked together with olive oil. SERVES 4 TO 6

several splashes of olive oil
1 eggplant, cut into 1-inch (2.5 cm)
    chunks
a few zucchini, cut into 1-inch (2.5 cm)
    chunks
1 red bell pepper, cored and seeded,
    cut into 1-inch (2.5 cm) chunks
1 green bell pepper, cored and seeded,
    cut into 1-inch (2.5 cm) chunks
a few onions, sliced
4 or 5 cloves of garlic, finely chopped

several garden ripe tomatoes, cut into
    1-inch (2.5 cm) chunks or one 28 oz
    (796 mL) can of whole tomatoes
a bay leaf
a few sprigs of fresh thyme or 1 tea-
    spoon (5 mL) of dried
a sprinkle or two of sea salt and freshly
    ground pepper
1 or 2 bunches of fresh basil, chopped
1 tablespoon (15 mL) of balsamic
    vinegar

Begin by sautéing the eggplant and zucchini in a large skillet over high heat with a splash or two of olive oil. Continue cooking, stirring and toss-ing, until the vegetables are golden brown and tender, 10 minutes or so. Set these vegetables aside in a bowl.

There are as many ways to make rata-touille as there are cooks, all with the same basic group of ingredients. The easiest method is to simply pile every-thing into a stockpot and simmer until tender. While this is a perfectly appro-priate way to make a vegetable stew, it's not the tastiest way. For maximum flavour try it this way.

Turn the heat down a bit and con-tinue with another splash or two of olive oil and the bell peppers, cook-ing them just until they're tender, another 5 minutes or so. Add them to the first batch of reserved vegetables.

Next, sauté the onions with another splash of olive oil until they soften a bit. Add the garlic and continue for another few minutes.

Lower the heat. Add the tomatoes, bay leaf and thyme and simmer until the mixture thickens, another 10 minutes or so. Break up the whole tomatoes into smaller pieces.

Add the reserved vegetables and season the works with salt and pepper. Simmer until everything is heated through.

Stir in the fresh basil and balsamic vinegar and serve immediately.

You may finish the ratatouille with several heaping spoonfuls of freshly made Basil Pesto (page 246), fresh oregano, lots of sliced green onions or parsley. For a more Mediter-ranean flavour, try adding lots of kalamata-style black olives or arti-choke hearts. You can add a deli-cious grilled flavour to ratatouille by grilling the eggplant, zucchini and peppers and tossing them with the stewed tomato mixture and basil.

STEAKHOUSE MUSHROOM STEW

The rich meaty flavour of mushrooms makes them one of the most popular side dishes in any steakhouse. This richly flavoured side dish is also perfect with a simple green salad or a freshly baked potato, or tossed with pasta. SERVES 4

1 lb (500 g) or so of mixed mushrooms
½ stick (¼ cup/60 mL) of butter
2 onions, peeled and sliced
4 cloves of garlic, minced
1 bunch of fresh thyme, chopped,
   or 1 tablespoon (15 mL) of dried

a sprinkle or two of sea salt and freshly
   ground pepper
a splash or two of any red wine
½ cup (125 mL) of heavy cream (35%)
2 green onions, thinly sliced

Trim the mushrooms as needed, removing any tough stems. Cut the larger mushrooms into smaller pieces. Smaller mushrooms may be left whole or simply halved to show off their form. Rinse all the mushrooms well and roll them in a tea towel to dry them off.

Preheat a large skillet over medium-high heat and add the butter, onions and garlic. Sauté until the onions just begin to turn golden brown. Add the mushrooms and continue. In a few minutes the mushrooms will release quite a bit of moisture and become a bit soupy.

Add the thyme and salt and pepper. Continue cooking until the mushrooms are tender and most of the moisture has evaporated, concentrating the flavour. Add your choice of wine or spirit (see Variation) and the cream. Continue simmering until the sauce has thickened once again. Stir in the green onions.

You may use any combination of mushrooms—shiitake, oyster, portabella, button or cremini—or just a single variety to make this dish. For the liquor, you may use sherry, port, brandy, Madeira or Marsala. For the herbs, try using rosemary or tarragon instead of thyme, and dried herbs are fine if you don't have fresh.

MAPLE MASHED SWEET POTATOES

This dish is on my table's top-ten list, and not just because it's easy to make and tastes great. Sweet potatoes are one of the healthiest vegetables you can eat. They're packed with a laundry list of nutrients and always taste great, especially with aromatic olive oil instead of rich butter. SERVES 4 TO 6

4 sweet potatoes (unpeeled)
1 cup (250 mL) of maple syrup
¼ cup (60 mL) of olive oil

a sprinkle or two of sea salt and
  freshly ground pepper
2 green onions, minced

Bake the sweet potatoes at 400°F (200°C) until they're tender and soft, 45 minutes or so.

Toss the unpeeled baked sweet potatoes into a bowl and splash in the maple syrup and olive oil. Mash well and then season with salt and pepper. Stir in the green onions and serve immediately.

You may remove the skins if you like; you'll lose some nutrients but not enough to really matter. Try tossing in some of your favourite fresh herb: thyme, tarragon, cilantro, oregano, basil, chives and parsley all work very well.

SWEET POTATO ALOO GOBI

In India, aloo gobi *means "potato cauliflower": it's one of their most common vegetable dishes. It's one of my family's favourites too, partly because it's so easy to make, but mostly because it's full of so much addictive bright flavour. It's normally made with plain white potatoes and cauliflower, but, for even more colour, flavour and nutrition, this version uses sweet potatoes instead.*

SERVES 4 TO 6

½ stick (¼ cup/60 mL) of butter
1 tablespoon (15 mL) of whole
    cumin seeds
2 onions, diced
2 teaspoons (10 mL) of ground
    cinnamon
2 tablespoons (30 mL) of curry powder

2 large sweet potatoes, peeled and cut
    into 1-inch (2.5 cm) chunks
1 head of cauliflower, cut into florets
a sprinkle or two of sea salt
a splash or two of water
1 cup (250 mL) of frozen peas
1 bunch of cilantro, chopped

Freestyle VARIATION

You may toss in a few sliced green onions along with the cilantro. If you're not a fan of cilantro, simply leave it out. For a more authentic version, try substituting regular potatoes for the sweet potatoes. Feel free to adjust the amount of spices to suit your taste. If you enjoy a bit of spicy heat, try stirring in all or part of a minced jalapeño pepper.

Melt the butter in a large skillet over medium heat. Add the cumin seeds and gently fry them for a minute or two to heat them through, remove any shelf staleness and brighten their flavour.

Add the onions and sauté until they soften. Add the cinnamon and curry powder and stir well for another minute or so. The direct heat of the sauté dramatically brightens the flavours of the spices.

Add the sweet potato chunks and cauliflower florets and stir or toss well to coat them with the spices.

Season with salt, add a splash or two of water, cover with a tight-fitting lid and lower the heat. Continue cooking until the sweet potatoes are tender, another 20 minutes or so.

Just before serving, stir in the peas and cilantro, quickly heating them through.

TREATS & BAKED GOODIES

COUNTRY BREAD, CITY BREAD

This is the tastiest bread I have ever made. It's also the easiest because the secret ingredient in all true bread is time, not laborious kneading. The key to an addictive loaf of rich, hearty goodness is an overnight rest for the living dough. With time, water and flour naturally form an elastic dough that rises with just a small amount of yeast. Here's how to make your own Country Bread, full of rustic whole grain goodness, or a loaf of refined white City Bread. MAKES 1 LOAF

FOR A LOAF OF COUNTRY BREAD
3 cups (750 mL) of all-purpose flour
   or bread flour
1 cup (250 mL) of whole wheat flour
½ cup (125 mL) of any multi-grain mix
   (see Variations below)
½ heaping teaspoon (2 mL)
   of active dry yeast
2 teaspoons (10 mL) of salt
2¼ cups (560 mL) of warm water

FOR A LOAF OF CITY BREAD
5 cups (1.25 L) of all-purpose
   or bread flour
½ heaping teaspoon (2 mL)
   of active dry yeast
2 teaspoons (10 mL) of salt
2½ cups (625 mL) of warm water

Freestyle VARIATION

Bread flour has a higher concentration of gluten in it so it will produce the strongest loaf with the most rise. All-purpose flour has less gluten but will still produce a beautiful loaf of bread. In either case the dough is strong enough to hold lots of multi-grain bits so, in the Country Bread, for a multi-grain mix, you may use a blend such as Red River cereal or a 12-grain cereal breakfast blend. You may also use plain oatmeal, cornmeal or even potato flakes. For heartier Country Bread try 2 cups each of whole wheat and bread flours and ½ cup of any multi-grain mix.

In a large bowl whisk the dry ingredients together, evenly distributing the salt and yeast throughout the flour. Pour in the warm water and stir with the handle of a wooden spoon until a moist dough forms. Continue stirring vigorously until the dough incorporates all the loose flour in the bowl, 1 or 2 minutes in total.

Cover the bowl with plastic wrap and let rest in a warm place for 12 to 14 hours. The dough will double in size and bubble, and long elastic gluten strands will form naturally without laborious kneading.

Dust the dough lightly with a bit of flour. Oil hands lightly and, with your fingertips, gather dough from the outside edges to the middle, knocking it down into a loose ball. Turn out onto a lightly floured board and knead for a few moments until a tight ball forms. Toss the ball back in the bowl and lightly coat with a splash of vegetable oil, turning to evenly cover.

Gently roll the dough into a thick log that fits end to end in a lightly oiled 9- × 5-inch (2 L) loaf pan and, without covering, rest it a second time. In 2 to 3 hours it will double in size once more.

Meanwhile, preheat your oven to 425°F (220°C). When the dough is ready, bake for 45 minutes.

FROZEN BUTTER BISCUITS

These are my gold standard biscuits. Their secret? Frozen butter! It's an old pastry chef's trick that has served me well. Butter tastes great, and the moisture in it helps the biscuits rise. Also, when it's frozen, butter is very easy to shred into the dough. After you try these a few times, you'll be able to bake them in under 20 minutes—and clean up the mess too! MAKES 8 TO 10 LARGE BISCUITS

4 cups (1 L) of all-purpose flour
2 tablespoons (30 mL)
    of baking powder
2 teaspoons (10 mL) of salt

2 sticks (1 cup/250 mL)
    of frozen butter
1½ cups (375 mL) of milk
a sprinkle or two of sea salt and freshly
    ground pepper

Preheat your oven to 400°F (200°C).

Whisk the flour, baking powder and salt together until they're evenly mixed. Using a standard box or potato grater, grate the frozen butter into the flour and toss lightly with your fingers until it's thoroughly combined. Because the butter is frozen, it grates into tiny pieces that don't bond with the flour; they stay separate and help make the biscuits light and fluffy.

Pour the milk into the flour mixture, and stir with the handle end of a wooden spoon to form a dough mass. The spoon's handle is gentler on the dough than its bowl. Fold the dough over a few times with your hands until all the ingredients come together. If necessary add a few more spoonfuls of milk to help gather up any stray flour.

Pat the dough out on a lightly floured cutting board to form a loose round shape. Cut the round into wedges—like a pie—or any other shape you're in the mood for. Position pieces on a baking sheet and sprinkle with a bit of coarse salt and coarsely ground pepper.

Bake for 15 minutes or so. You'll know they're done when they turn golden brown.

Folding the dough in this way strengthens the dough a bit but not enough to toughen the biscuits. It also helps form crisp crusts when they bake. Too much kneading creates the stretchy gluten that makes bread strong—and biscuits tough. For maximum tenderness, though, avoid overworking the dough.

Biscuits are easily scented with herbs and spices. A spoonful or so adds lots of flavour. I tend to use aromatics that reflect the rest of the meal but, really, anything goes. Add caraway seeds to biscuits for beef stew or add a touch of nutmeg to breakfast biscuits. Rosemary, thyme and even curry powder all taste great too.

CINNAMON ROLLS

Few things say "Good Morning" better than a batch of warm-from-the-oven cinnamon rolls! You can bake them with speedy baking powder, but an old-school yeast dough always has the best texture and flavour. MAKES 12 TO 16 ROLLS

SWEET DOUGH

1 cup (250 mL) of milk

1 stick (½ cup/125 mL) of butter, softened

½ cup (125 mL) of brown sugar

2 tablespoons (30 mL) of pure vanilla extract

1 teaspoon (5 mL) of salt

5 cups (1.25 L) of all-purpose flour

one ¼ oz (8 g) package of instant yeast

4 eggs

CINNAMON FILLING

1 stick (½ cup/125 mL) of butter, softened

1 cup (250 mL) of brown sugar

2 tablespoons (30 mL) of ground cinnamon

GLAZE

1 cup (250 mL) of powdered sugar

¼ cup (60 mL) of heavy cream (35%)

1 tablespoon (15 mL) of pure vanilla extract

For an extra special burst of aromatic flavour, add the zest of several oranges into the sweet dough.

For the sweet dough, gently warm the milk, butter, brown sugar, vanilla and salt in a small pot. Stir until everything melts together.

Meanwhile, measure half of the flour into the bowl of your stand mixer along with the yeast. Add the warm milk mixture to the flour and beat with your paddle attachment until smooth. Add the eggs 1 at a time, beating until smooth before proceeding. Switch to a dough hook and add the remaining flour.

Remove and knead until a soft dough forms that is no longer sticky to the touch, about 5 minutes. Place the dough in a lightly oiled bowl, cover and let rest in a warm place until dough doubles in size, up to 2 hours.

For the filling, stir or whisk together the softened butter with the brown sugar and the cinnamon in a mixing bowl.

Once the dough has risen, knock it down and let it rest for a few minutes.

Flour your work surface, the dough, your hands and a rolling pin. Roll out the dough into a long rectangle shape, about 18 × 12 inches (45 × 30 cm).

Evenly spread the cinnamon filling all over the top of the dough, leaving 1 or 2 inches (2.5 or 5 cm) uncovered along the top edge. Leaving a border helps the dough stick together when you form the roll.

Roll into a long, tight, cigar-shaped log from the covered long edge to the uncovered long edge. Brush the outside of the log with oil or melted butter.

Slice the dough log into 12 or 16 sections. Turn each on its side and position evenly in a lightly oiled 15- × 10-inch (38 × 25 cm) baking pan.

Rest, uncovered, until the dough doubles in size once again and the rolls swell into each other, filling the pan.

Meanwhile, preheat your oven to 350°F (180°C).

When the dough has risen a second time, bake for 40 to 45 minutes.

When the cinnamon rolls have cooled enough to handle, stir together the glaze ingredients and drizzle all over the rolls. Serve immediately!

BREAD PUDDING

Bread pudding is a simple way to transform stale bread into a wide variety of simple treats. Bread puddings are versatile, easy to make and supremely tasty. They are one of my favourite comfort foods. SERVES 8

1 lb (500 g) of stale bread,
    cut into cubes
1 cup (250 mL) of raisins or other
    dried fruit
3 cups (750 mL) of milk
4 eggs

1 cup (250 mL) of brown or
    white sugar
1 teaspoon (5 mL) of ground cinnamon
    or your favourite baking spice
1 tablespoon (15 mL) of pure
    vanilla extract
2 tablespoons (30 mL) of coarse sugar

Preheat your oven to 350°F (180°C).

Toss the bread and raisins into a large bowl.

In a separate bowl, whisk together the milk, eggs, your choice of sweetener, your favourite spice and the vanilla. Pour the mixture over the bread and stir until the bread is coated. At first, the bread will float on the milk mixture, but after a few minutes it will begin to absorb it and sink.

Let rest for 15 minutes or so and then pour it into a 9-inch (23 cm) square lightly greased ovenproof casserole dish. Sprinkle coarse sugar overtop and bake until the eggs set, the pudding firms and the top is golden brown, about 1 hour.

For lots of extra flavour, take the time to toast the bread until golden brown. For an extra special touch, try using challah, brioche or croissants. You may use honey or maple syrup instead of sugar, and you may replace the cinnamon with the baking spice of your choice. Ground cardamom, nutmeg, ginger, allspice or cloves all work well. You can also stir in 1 cup (250 mL) of chocolate chips. Or, for even more chocolate flavour, you can substitute 1 cup (250 mL) of heavy cream (35%) for the 1 cup (250 mL) of milk, and melt 12 oz (375 g) of dark chocolate into it.

PANNA COTTA

I don't have a pastry chef on staff at my house so I'm always on the lookout for an easy-to-make dessert like panna cotta. In Italian, the name panna cotta *simply means cooked milk. This treat is smooth and light and can be flavoured with any herb, spice or liqueur. It's so simple to make that it'll become part of your repertoire the first time you make it.* MAKES 6

4 cups (1 L) of milk
1 cup (250 mL) of white or
    brown sugar
2 teaspoons (10 mL) of pure
    vanilla extract

1 tablespoon (15 mL) of your favourite
    spice or herb or a splash of your
    favourite liqueur
2 packages unflavoured gelatin (about
    2½ teaspoons/12 mL each)

Freestyle VARIATION

Instead of the white or brown sugar, you may use honey or maple syrup. One of my favourite savoury flavourings for panna cotta is a bit of minced rosemary. Its woodsy flavour is perfectly enhanced by the vanilla. Spiced rum, Grand Marnier, nutmeg and saffron are all tasty too.

Pour almost all of the milk into a small saucepot and gently warm it over medium heat. Stir in the sugar, vanilla and spices or liqueur. Continue heating until the mixture just begins to simmer.

Meanwhile, sprinkle the gelatin powder over the remaining milk. Let it rest for a minute or two to allow the gelatin to begin to rehydrate and absorb moisture. Pour in the hot milk mixture and stir until the gelatin is completely melted and dissolves into the mixture.

Divide the mixture evenly among 6 small dessert moulds. To help the panna cottas release easily, lightly oil the moulds before filling them. (Have fun with the moulds. Look around the house: teacups and ramekins work best but even Styrofoam and plastic cups trimmed to size work well too.)

Refrigerate until firm, at least 2 hours or overnight. To release the panna cotta from its mould, gently loosen the edges, cover with a small plate, then flip over. Don't worry about leftovers! There won't be any.

OLD-FASHIONED APPLE PIE

My favourite dessert is a thick slice of just-baked pie, with apples fresh from our local orchard, and still warm from the oven. But I'm always careful to save a thick wedge because I believe apple pie is at its best the next morning for breakfast. I prefer an easy-to-make butter pastry crust. Its secret is frozen butter, which adds flavour and is much easier than shortening to "cut" into the flour. SERVES 6 TO 8

PASTRY

2½ cups (625 mL) of all-purpose flour
2 tablespoons (30 mL) of white sugar
1 teaspoon (5 mL) of salt
2 sticks (1 cup/250 mL) of
　　frozen butter
12 tablespoons (180 mL) of ice water

FILLING

6 or 8 large Honey Crisp or
　　Granny Smith apples, peeled,
　　cored and sliced
½ cup (125 mL) of brown sugar
2 tablespoons (30 mL) of
　　all-purpose flour
1 teaspoon (5 mL) of ground cinnamon

Whisk the flour, sugar and salt together in a large bowl.

Using a standard box or potato grater, grate the frozen butter into the flour and toss lightly with your fingers until it's thoroughly combined. Sprinkle in the ice water and stir with your fingers, mixing and firmly kneading until the dough comes together in a ball.

Divide dough into 2 pieces; making sure that one half is slightly larger than the other. Wrap in plastic wrap, flatten and chill for at least 30 minutes, or even overnight. Resting tenderizes the pastry, making it easier to roll.

Remove the pastry from the refrigerator and allow it to warm slightly, just until it's pliable. Lightly flour your hands, the rolling pin, your work surface and the dough.

Roll out the larger pastry piece into a circle large enough to slightly overlap the edges of a 9-inch (23 cm) glass deep-dish pie dish. As you roll, for ease of handling, lightly flour the dough every time its diameter doubles, then flip it over and continue rolling. Transfer the dough to the pie dish by folding it into quarters, then unfolding it in the dish.

Preheat your oven to 375°F (190°C).

Toss the apple slices with the brown sugar, flour and cinnamon. Add the apple mixture to the bottom crust. Roll out the remaining smaller piece and carefully place it over the top of the pie.

Roll and crimp the edges of the dough together, tightly sealing them. Poke a few vent holes into the top of the pie and place on the bottom rack of your oven. Bake for an hour or so, until the crust is golden and the juices are bubbling.

You may use any apples of your choice and, for extra flavour, try tossing the apples with 1 cup (250 mL) or so of raisins. For another seasonal treat, try substituting 2½ lb (1.25 kg) of peeled and sliced ripe local peaches for the apples.

FRUIT CRISP

All over the world, one of the simplest ways to turn a pile of ripe fruit into a warm comfortable dessert is to slowly bake them with aromatic spices under an easy-to-make crumbly crust. SERVES 6 TO 8

2 to 3 lb (1 to 1.5 kg) of your choice of fruit (see Variation below)
1 teaspoon (5 mL) of ground cinnamon
1 cup (250 mL) of all-purpose flour

1 cup (250 mL) of brown or white sugar
1 teaspoon (5 mL) of nutmeg
1 stick (½ cup/125 mL) of butter, melted

Preheat your oven to 350°F (180°C).

Toss the fruit with the cinnamon, then spread it evenly into a 9- × 5-inch (2 L) baking pan 2 inches (5 cm) deep.

In a mixing bowl, whisk together the flour, sugar and nutmeg. Drizzle in the melted butter and stir until well blended with the dry ingredients.

Scatter this topping evenly over the top of the fruit. Bake until fruit juices are bubbling around the edges, the fruit is tender and the top is golden brown, about 1 hour.

There are many ways to add your own freestyle ideas to a fruit crisp. Try apples, peaches, pears, plums, pineapple (peeled, cored and cut into chunks), rhubarb or banana chunks, or any berry. Even chunks of mango bake into a memorable crisp. You may use one fruit or try different combinations of fruit. If you choose berries, it's best to toss them with a spoonful or two of flour to help soak up their extra juices. You may also try stirring in raisins or your favourite nuts. You can modify the topping with whole wheat flour and vegetable oil instead of white flour and butter. You can use your favourite baking spice instead of cinnamon or nutmeg. Cardamom is always a treat!

CHOCOLATE CHIP COOKIES

Every kitchen needs a gold standard recipe for chocolate chip cookies. This one has earned its stripes under fire, over many seasons, through countless licked spoons, spilled vanilla and extra chips in the batter. Its quick baking time is the key to addictively chewy cookies that friends and family won't be able to resist. MAKES ABOUT 18 COOKIES (DEPENDING ON SIZE)

1½ cups (375 mL) of all-purpose flour
1 teaspoon (5 mL) of baking powder
¼ teaspoon (1 mL) of salt
1 stick (½ cup/125 mL) of butter, softened

1 cup (250 mL) of brown sugar
1 egg
1 teaspoon (5 mL) of pure vanilla extract
1 cup (250 mL) of chocolate chips

For a richer chocolate flavour, add 1 tablespoon (15 mL) of cocoa powder to the dry ingredients. For an extra special treat, substitute M&M's for the chips. You may also stir in 1 cup (250 mL) of pine nuts. If you prefer less molasses flavour, substitute white sugar for half the brown sugar.

Preheat your oven to 375°F (190°C).

Whisk the flour, baking powder and salt together and set aside.

Using a stand mixer or a food processor, cream the butter and sugar together until smooth. If you don't have a stand mixer, beat vigorously by hand in a large mixing bowl.

Add the egg and vanilla and continue beating until well combined. Scrape down the bowl and gradually add the flour mixture, beating just until combined. Stir in the chocolate chips.

Using a spoon, scoop out a ball of the dough, roll it for a moment in your hands and then drop it onto a lightly greased cookie tray. Slightly flatten the balls but leave lots of room in between to allow the cookies room to expand.

For a soft, chewy cookie, bake for exactly 12 minutes. For a cookie with a bit of crispy crunch, bake for exactly 15 minutes.

Cool for 2 minutes on the cookie sheet and then remove and cool further.

TRIPLE CHOCOLATE BROWNIES

When we crave a rich decadent chocolate treat, guess who gets sent to the kitchen to bake these rich, chewy, dark chocolate brownies? Their amazing flavour is quick and easy to get in the oven and an absolutely essential part of any kitchen's repertoire! MAKES 12 LARGE BROWNIES OR 16 TO 24 SMALLER ONES

8 oz (250 g) of dark chocolate
2 sticks (1 cup/250 mL) of butter
1 cup (250 mL) of all-purpose flour
½ cup (125 mL) of cocoa powder
1 teaspoon (5 mL) of baking powder
a pinch of salt

4 eggs
2 cups (500 mL) of brown sugar
1 tablespoon (15 mL) of pure
  vanilla extract
1 cup (250 mL) of chocolate chips

These are a moist fudgy-style brownie. For a more cake-like version, add an extra ½ cup (125 mL) of flour to the batter. For a sophisticated flavour boost, add the zest of several oranges into the batter.

Preheat your oven to 350°F (180°C).

To protect the chocolate from direct heat, melt it and the butter in a heat-proof bowl set over a small pot of simmering water, stirring constantly. When the chocolate and butter have melted, whisk until smooth.

While the chocolate mixture cools slightly, whisk together the flour, cocoa powder, baking powder and salt. Add the eggs, sugar and vanilla to the chocolate and mix thoroughly. Stir in the flour mixture and chocolate chips until incorporated.

Pour batter into a lightly oiled and floured 9- × 13-inch (3.5 L) pan. Bake for exactly 25 minutes.

MOLTEN CHOCOLATE CAKES

An individual chocolate cake with a molten runny centre is the ultimate dinner party treat. Slightly underbaking the batter makes each cake come out with its own special sauce hidden inside. MAKES 6 TO 8 CAKES

8 oz (250 g) of top-quality bittersweet
   or dark chocolate
1 stick (½ cup/125 mL) of butter,
   softened
2 tablespoons (30 mL) of cocoa
   powder
4 eggs
¼ cup (60 mL) of brown or white sugar

1 tablespoon (15 mL) of pure
   vanilla extract
butter for greasing ramekins
white sugar for sprinkling on
   greased ramekins
heavy cream, whipped, or ice cream,
   for serving

Preheat your oven to 400°F (200°C).

To protect the chocolate from direct heat, melt it and the butter in a heat-proof bowl set over a pot of simmering water, gently stirring until the butter and chocolate melt together. Remove from the heat and sift in the cocoa powder, stirring until smooth.

Meanwhile, beat the eggs with the brown sugar and vanilla until they are thick and smooth. Pour in the melted chocolate and stir until smooth.

Rub the inside of each ramekin or muffin mould with butter to make a thin film. Lightly sprinkle each with sugar and shake to coat the inside, shaking out any excess. Evenly divide the cake batter among the ramekins.

Place on a rimmed baking sheet and bake until the batter rises, the tops are cracked and the insides are still a bit gooey, no more than 10 minutes.

Cool for a few minutes; the cakes will shrink a bit and pull away from the sides. If necessary, run a paring knife around the edges of the cakes to loosen them. Carefully invert onto a plate. Serve with lots of whipped cream or ice cream.

For an even more elegant flavour, add the zest of a few oranges into the batter. For a completely different effect—molten vanilla cakes—try using white chocolate and doubling the amount of vanilla.

JARS

BASIL PESTO

This is the classic Pesto Genovese featuring basil, pine nuts and Parmesan cheese. It's a perfect accompaniment for white meats, fish or pasta. Because the word pesto *simply means "paste," you can use many different ingredient combinations to make this tasty condiment.* MAKES ABOUT 1 CUP (250 ML)

a few large handfuls of fresh basil
½ cup (125 mL) or so of grated Parmesan or
    Romano cheese
a few handfuls of pine nuts
a generous splash or two of your best extra
    virgin olive oil
a sprinkle or two of salt and pepper

Toss everything into a food processor and purée until smooth. The olive oil's job is to help get everything spinning in the food processor. Because it also adds flavour, this is a good place to use your very best oil.

freestyleVARIATION

Toss in a few garlic cloves for pungent strength. Try experimenting with different herb, cheese and nut combinations such as mint, goat cheese and pistachio, or sage, goat cheese and walnut.

CHIMICHURRI

Chimichurri is a spicy, vinegar-spiked, pesto-like condiment from Argentina, where it's used both as a sauce and a marinade for meat. Its bright flavours reflect the combination of Spanish and Italian influences. It's one of the world's great condiments and a great way to add a touch of authentic flair to any grilled meat or fish. You may serve or use as a marinade immediately, but this condiment is at its best after a day or two of refrigeration. MAKES ABOUT 2 CUPS (500 ML)

a bunch of parsley
a bunch of cilantro
2 tablespoons (30 mL) of chopped fresh
    oregano
4 cloves of garlic
½ jalapeño pepper, seeded
¼ cup (60 mL) of red wine vinegar
½ cup (125 mL) or so of olive oil
a sprinkle or two of sea salt

Toss the herbs, garlic, jalapeño pepper and red wine vinegar into a food processor and purée until coarsely chopped. While the food processor is running, pour in the olive oil until a creamy yet chunky sauce forms. Add salt to taste.

freestyleVARIATION

Try adding an onion or a spoonful of ground cumin for even more flavour.

CLOCKWISE FROM TOP LEFT: Homemade Ketchup, Pickled Red Onions, Butterscotch Sauce, Cinnamon Applesauce, Basil Pesto, Spicy Thai Peanut Sauce, Chimichurri, Dark Chocolate Sauce, Spicy Fresh Salsa, and Cocktail Sauce (in centre)

PICKLED RED ONIONS

These tasty onions lose all their pungency in the pickling process but gain a sweet sharpness that makes them a great last-minute addition to any salad. They're also delicious served as a condiment with any type of fish or meat. They're a true multi-purpose condiment! MAKES ABOUT 2 CUPS (500 ML)

2 large red onions
1 cup (250 mL) of sugar
1 cup (250 mL) of red wine vinegar
a sprinkle or two of salt and pepper

Slice the onions as thinly as possible. You may find it useful to first slice them in half and lay them on their cut side before slicing them further. Cram the sliced onions into a large Mason jar.

Pour the sugar and red wine vinegar into a small pot and bring to a boil with the salt and pepper. Add the onions and continue heating just long enough to return the mixture to a simmer.

Pour the mixture into the Mason jar, cover it and rest overnight in the refrigerator before use.

Because sugar and vinegar are such great preservatives, these pickled onions will last indefinitely in your refrigerator. They're at their best after a day or two in your fridge, once their flavours have had a chance to mature.

freestyle VARIATION

You may aromatize the pickling liquid with a spoonful of your favourite herb or spice. Try bay leaves, fennel seed or even ground juniper berries. For a very aromatic version, try adding a spoonful or two of standard pickling spice to the simmering sugar before adding the onions.

SPICY FRESH SALSA

A jar packed with freshly tossed salsa, full of juicy ripe tomatoes and aromatic flavours, is easy to make and easy to enjoy. Sweet tomatoes, pungent onions, sour limes, aromatic herbs, salt and spicy pepper all balance each other in a vibrant harmony of tastes. A good salsa doesn't ruin your day with too much spicy heat; it brightens it with just enough. MAKES 2 CUPS (500 ML)

2 or 3 ripe local tomatoes, finely chopped
1 chili pepper, minced
1 bunch of chopped cilantro
zest and juice of 1 or 2 limes
a big splash of your best olive oil
1 teaspoon (5 mL) of tomato paste
1 teaspoon (5 mL) of ground cumin
a sprinkle or two of salt

Toss everything together in a bowl until well combined.

Garden tomatoes have the most flavour—when they're in season. If they're not, look for organic or vine-attached types, take them home and ripen them for a few days on a sunny windowsill. In a pinch, a small can of whole tomatoes is more flavourful than a few hard unripe ones and will add lots of deep, rich tomato flavour.

freestyle VARIATION

There are many types of chili peppers, each with its own heat level and flavour. I prefer medium heat varieties like poblano and jalapeño. You may substitute chili peppers with freshly grated ginger. Cilantro is the classic fresh herb in salsa, but basil, oregano and even parsley work well too. The sweet pungency of a red onion is a great replacement for the green onions. You can save some time by tossing everything into your food processor. The colour will be a bit dark but the results will still taste great.

HOMEMADE KETCHUP

If you like ketchup as much as I do, you'll love this recipe for homemade ketchup. It's packed with so much aromatic goodness that you'll wonder why you ever used store-bought. It's the best way to jazz up a burger and fries and feel good all the other times you reach for ketchup! MAKES 4 CUPS (1 L)

one 28 oz (796 mL) can of chopped tomatoes
one 5.5 oz (156 mL) can of tomato paste
1 large onion, chopped
1 cup (250 mL) of red wine vinegar
½ cup (125 mL) of sugar
½ cup (125 mL) of olive oil
2 tablespoons (30 mL) of ground nutmeg
½ teaspoon (2 mL) of ground allspice
2 or 3 bay leaves
a sprinkle or two of salt and pepper

Toss all the ingredients into a large saucepan. Place over medium heat and bring to a simmer. Continue cooking, stirring occasionally, until the mixture reduces by half, about 30 minutes.

Here's a trick to determine whether a liquid has reduced by half. In this recipe, stand a wooden spoon in the pot and mark the ketchup's level on it. Use that mark as a reference to know when the mixture has reduced by half.

Cool the ketchup to room temperature (an agitated hot liquid always expands violently; it'll explode all over your kitchen and make a huge mess), and then purée the mixture in a food process, blender or in the pot using an immersion blender.

Get some French fries and start dipping!

freestyle VARIATION
If you're a fan of garlic, toss a whole head of peeled cloves into the pot. After the sauce is reduced, try adding your favourite hot sauce until the ketchup is pleasingly spicy.

COCKTAIL SAUCE

This brightly flavoured condiment traditionally highlights the delicate flavours of fish with the energetic punch of sharp horseradish and bright lemon. Try it. You'll forget you ever met its bland, sugar-laden, store-bought cousins. MAKES 1 LARGE JAR (ABOUT 4 CUPS / 1 LITRE)

one 28 oz (796 mL) can of whole ripe tomatoes
one 5.5 oz (156 mL) can of tomato paste
several large heaping spoonfuls of horseradish
zest and juice of 2 lemons
2 tablespoons (30 mL) of Worcestershire
    sauce
as much Tabasco sauce as you like
a sprinkle or two of salt

Blend everything in a food processor or blender. Not too smooth though; leave it slightly chunky.

freestyle VARIATION
Unless it's tomato season in my backyard, I prefer the field-ripe flavour of canned tomatoes to the bland hardness of their fresh cousins. For a touch of complementary herb flavour, add a handful of minced fresh dill, cilantro or basil.

SPICY THAI PEANUT SAUCE

This all-purpose condiment is a great way to add a splash of Thai flavour to a salad or vegetable dish. The secret to its exotic flavour is its perfect balance of sweet, sour, salty and spicy. MAKES ABOUT 2 CUPS (500 ML)

½ cup (125 mL) of smooth peanut butter
zest and juice of 4 limes
¼ cup (60 mL) of honey
¼ cup (60 mL) of soy sauce
¼ cup (60 mL) of water
1 teaspoon (5 mL) of chili flakes or hot sauce
a large bunch of mint
a handful or two of peanuts

Toss everything into your food processor or blender, then purée until almost smooth, leaving the peanuts a touch chunky. Some blenders are stronger than others; if yours needs a little help, add a splash of water to help it purée to a thick peanut butter consistency.

freestyleVARIATION

If you like the strong flavour of fresh cilantro, use it to replace some, or all, of the mint. For even more authentic Thai flavour, add a splash of Thai fish sauce.

BUTTERSCOTCH SAUCE

This classic turns anything into an instant treat with its deep caramel flavour. Every time I transform bland white sugar into rich, slightly bitter caramel, I get excited. It's just magical how much flavour a simple cooking process can add! MAKES 2 CUPS (500 ML)

1 cup (250 mL) of water
1 cup (250 mL) of white sugar
1 stick (½ cup/125 mL) of butter,
    cut into pieces
1 cup (250 mL) of heavy cream (35%)
a splash of pure vanilla extract

Pour the water into a saucepan. Add the sugar in a small, tight pile in the centre of the water. Begin heating over a high heat. Don't stir! The water and sugar will quickly dissolve together and form simple syrup.

As the heat continues to rise, the sugar will start to turn pale golden. When you see the first hint of colour, gently swirl the pan to keep the colour even.

Water helps the sugar dissolve and melt evenly without getting grainy. Avoid stirring —it causes bits of sugar to splash on the side of the pot where they can dry, fall back into the syrup and turn the whole syrup gritty. As the heat increases, the sauce will simmer and steam, and the water will gradually evaporate. The steam will die down, and the temperature will begin to rise past the boiling point of water, leaving behind a pure melted sugar syrup.

When it's a deep golden brown, add the butter and whisk it in until the sauce is smooth. This will quickly drop the sauce's temperature and prevent it from over-browning.

Add the cream and vanilla and whisk until smooth. Pour into a jar and refrigerate until thickened.

freestyleVARIATION

For a touch of grown-up flavour, you may add a splash of your favourite rum or liqueur to the sauce before cooling it.

CINNAMON APPLESAUCE

In the fall, when apples are in peak season, I always make a giant batch or two of apple-sauce and freeze it. It's one of my favourite things to do in the kitchen with my son, Gabe. MAKES 4 CUPS (1 L)

a dozen or so of your favourite apples
1 cup (250 mL) of brown sugar
1 heaping tablespoon (15 mL)
    of ground cinnamon
a dash of pure vanilla extract
a dash of salt
a splash of water

Remove the cores from the apples but leave the skins on. Cut them into large chunks.

Toss into a pot and add the brown sugar, cinnamon, vanilla and salt. Add a splash of water, just enough to cover the bottom of the pot, and place over a medium-high heat.

Cover with a tight-fitting lid. In a few minutes the water will begin to steam, and the heat will encourage the apples to soften and release their own moisture.

There are many types of apples; each behaves differently when cooked. Some will soften and break down quickly, others will take longer. Any apple makes great apple-sauce, but my favourites are McIntosh and Golden Delicious.

Keep an eye on the pot and stir frequently so they don't stick to the bottom. Cook until all the apples are softened and the mixture simmers, about 20 minutes in total.

For a rustic chunky consistency, pass the sauce through a food mill or force it through a colander with the back of a spoon. For a smoother version, purée in a food processor and then pass through a strainer. In either case the skins will be left behind and should be discarded.

freestyle VARIATION
Many spices have an affinity for apples. Try nutmeg, allspice, cloves or cardamom. Some herbs are very tasty too. I enjoy rosemary, thyme and even bay leaf.

DARK CHOCOLATE SAUCE

Commercial chocolate sauces are a pale imitation of the real thing and usually don't include any real chocolate. An old-school batch of real chocolate sauce is easy to make, easy to use and an easy way to saturate any treat with lots of rich, true, chocolate flavour. Try not to eat too much of this sauce straight out of the jar! MAKES 2 CUPS (500 ML)

1 cup (250 mL) of heavy cream (35%)
2 tablespoons (30 mL) of sugar
2 tablespoons (30 mL) of cocoa powder
8 oz (250 g) of bittersweet chocolate
1 teaspoon (5 mL) of pure vanilla extract

Pour the cream and sugar into a small sauce-pan and bring to a rolling boil, stirring con-stantly. Turn off the heat and whisk in the cocoa powder and chocolate, stirring until smooth. Whisk in the vanilla, pour into a jar and refrigerate.

freestyle VARIATION
For a sophisticated grown-up taste, you may substitute any of your favourite liqueurs: rum, brandy or cognac for the vanilla.

INDEX

THANKS!

I am blessed to be a part of an amazing team of passionate people who believe in what we do as much as I do. All of us have been engaged with the spirit of Chef at Home for years; all of us helped create this book.

Thank you Rachel and Gabe for inspiring me to be my best—in life and in the kitchen.

Thank you Gretha and Johanna, my partners, for our shared vision; Trevor for your inspired creativity, firm leadership and ongoing friendship. Thank you to everyone at Food Network Canada for continuing to believe in what we do.

Thank you Ann for your relentless leadership. Dean for seeing the light. Billie Jane for your poise and polish. Art, Rob, Johnny and Dennis for lugging all that production gear everywhere and Dugald for showing 'em where to put it! Thanks Tommy, Justin, Stanley and Maureen for the real cooking, and Patti for making it all look so easy. Thank you Erin for keeping us grounded and in touch with our fans. Thanks to Alana, Ann, Carla, Michaela and Jennifer. To Peter, Warren, Jim and Samafram for slicing and dicing me into a broadcast-ready fellow. And thanks to anybody who ever washed a dirty dish for me!

And most especially thank you—our audience—for supporting our genuine efforts. I'm humbled to share my food, my life, my show and this book with you.